between *us*

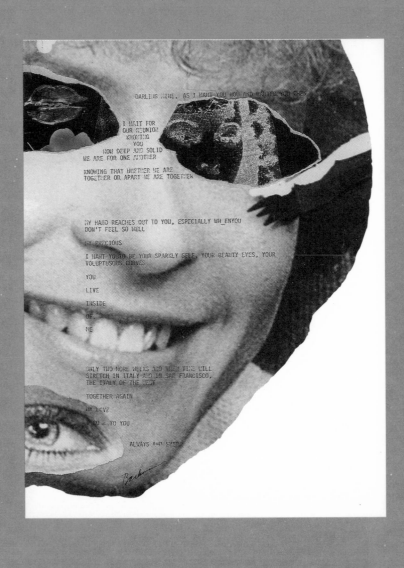

DARLING MINE, AS I WANT YOU NOW AND WANTED YOU THEN

I WAIT FOR
OUR REUNION
KNOWING
YOU
HOW DEEP AND SOLID
WE ARE FOR ONE ANOTHER

KNOWING THAT WHETHER WE ARE
TOGETHER OR APART WE ARE TOGETHER

MY HAND REACHES OUT TO YOU, ESPECIALLY WH_ENYOU
DON'T FEEL SO WELL

MY PRECIOUS

I WANT YOUTO BE YOUR SPARKLY SELF, YOUR BEAUTY EYES, YOUR
VOLUPTUSOUS CURVES

YOU

LIVE

INSIDE

OF

ME

ONLY TWO MORE WEEKS AND THEN TIME WILL
STRETCH IN ITALY AND IN SAN FRANCISCO,
THE ITALY OF THE WEST

TOGETHER AGAIN

MY LOVE

GO ME TO YOU

ALWAYS AND EVERY

Sealed With A Kiss:
INTRODUCING LESBIAN
LOVE LETTERS

It was Sappho herself who first indicated the relationship between women and letters. In an ancient riddle attributed to her she asks: "What creature is it that is female in nature and hides in its womb unborn children who, although they are voiceless, speak to people far away?" She answers her own riddle: "The female creature is a letter. The unborn children are the letters [of the alphabet] it carries. And the letters, although they have no voices, speak to people far away, whomever they wish ..."[1] Sappho hints at lesbian possibilities in her word game. Even in a time so distant, "whomever they wish" might have been a woman receiving a love letter from another woman. Though her "letter" is forever lost, history attests to its legacy in the inscription of thousands of real love letters written between women.

The diverse selection of love letters presented here were written between women and variously document, preserve, and celebrate both the idea and the lived reality of lesbian love. While it is true that the love letter, for any lover, can be an act of urgency, it has often been an act of sheer necessity for the lesbian lover, a crucial mode of expression. For hundreds of years, letters have been our private and sometimes sole recourse for documenting our unique and transgressive love—and, until only recently, the primary written evidence of lesbian culture.

9

The lesbian love letter dares to practice honesty and passion; it must tell the truth or no truth will be told. Each is in some way a record in our *her*story of defiance: Long before the first button, poster, pamphlet, or book made claims for our liberation, the lesbian love letter cried out, "I love you, no matter what the world thinks."

I actively collected lesbian love letters, notes, postcards, and e-mail for a year and a half beginning in the summer of 1994. In that period I read over 5000 pieces of mail. My research, limited to the United States, took me to friends and strangers throughout the country to pore over letters and cards that were bundled and boxed, cherished and saved, in attics, archives, and libraries. Throughout the course of my research, I also read previously published letters in books by or about lesbians, such as Natalie Barney and Janet Flanner; I solicited letters through lesbian publications; and I lectured on my project at women's bookstores. Some of the original letters in this volume were written with fountain pen on Parisian hotel stationery in the 1930s or typed single-spaced on onion-skin in the 1960s; some were found on torn sheets of loose-leaf paper decorated with peace signs and women's symbols in the 1970s; and a few examples were downloaded from e-mail love affairs in the 1990s. Clearly, the letters demonstrate that passion and sexual desire flow quite freely from the lesbian pen. But not all of these letters are romantic and not all of them are nice; letters of break-ups, of unrequited love, and of the pain inflicted by homophobia are included as well.

It is a bit of a dare to attempt to wrestle love letters from lesbians. Some are more than willing, others are anxious and still require the protection of anonymity; some cannot bear the review process, and others maintain a trash and burn policy at the end of any relationship. In my pursuit I pleaded and hounded and had a ball as I went through a remarkable process of discovery.

The result was that I experienced both the anxiety and the joy of what can only be called an embarrassment of riches. The work of one woman collecting, even as doggedly as I have, can result in only a sampling of what exists in the shoe boxes—in some cases the suitcases—of love filled over time, with letters by countless lesbians across the world and across time. A lesbian love affair can produce a daunting number of trips to the mailbox. (Radclyffe Hall, for example, wrote over 500 letters to her mistress Souline in a period of less than five years.)

I do feel fortunate that the lesbian struggle for freedom and recognition in recent years makes it possible in 1996 to gather together a collection of letters that represents the variousness and vitality of our loving. This book would have been much more difficult to assemble ten years ago, probably impossible just twenty years ago. Not surprisingly, I had the easiest time gathering material from the post-liberation period, since the 1970s. But certainly my project speaks as much to what has been lost, burned, restricted, or otherwise denied as it testifies to what remains.

Readers will find a few famous lovers here, such as Radclyffe Hall, Gertrude Stein, Emily Dickinson, and Virginia Woolf, but this collection emphasizes the letterworks of the common lesbian, the ordinary women—nurses, teachers, soldiers, housekeepers, waitresses, computer programmers, and copy-editors—whose rhetoric of love reveals the pervasive reality of being lesbian. It is the ordinary dykes who have created and sustained lesbian culture in everyday life. And it is their love letters that reveal the emotional core—the emotional truth—of the lesbian experience. My work as a folklorist leads me to seek meaning in vernacular forms of expression, but this book also follows a course set by poets, such as Sappho, Adrienne Rich, and Judy Grahn, whose art valorizes the commonality and commonness of lesbian experience. Rich maintains: "It is, quite simply, the ordinary in women which will 'rise' in every sense of the word.... History has been embellished with extraordinary... 'uncommon,' and of course 'token' women whose lives have left the rest unchanged. The 'common woman' is in fact the embodiment of the extraordinary will-to-survive in millions of women, a life-force... "[2]

The power of the "life-force," the "will-to-survive" represented in "common" lesbian love was demonstrated several times to me during the course of this project. I will give a single, telling example. One piece published here comes from a cache of letters written in 1912 by Margaret to Louise, which was discovered hidden in an old picture frame purchased by Nancy Morgan's stepmother in the early 1960s. When Morgan came out twenty years later, her stepmother presented her with the letters as a gift. Those letters had been hidden years before, most likely by Louise, who must have hoped that they would someday fall into sympathetic hands. For enclosed in a corner of the picture frame she had left a note in the form of a quotation: "The courage of the commonplace is greater than the courage of the crisis."

This book of the commonplace both complements and contrasts with a veritable outpouring of letter volumes by women in recent years. The writer Doris Grumbach recently asserted that so many volumes of passionate letters between famous women have been published that they could constitute a genre. But generally the contents of these books are not called lesbian. For example, a recent and greatly anticipated volume, *One Art: The Letters of Elizabeth Bishop* (1994), provides an autobiography-like selection of the poet's correspondence without including a single letter to any of her lovers. Late in the era of our liberation, there is much continued—I must say—pussyfooting about who and what to call "lesbian" and why.

Even though "lesbian" has been removed from the category of psychological deviance in recent years, and even though it has been claimed proudly as a term of identity by thousands of women throughout the world, to be lesbian is still widely demonized as a perversion or a source of tabloid-style titillation. One can still be "accused" of being lesbian. It is, I think, the lingering fear of such accusation that to this day skews the publication of letters by women who love each other and extends a history of prejudice.

I have consciously named this collection entirely lesbian—a first of its kind to record publicly *as lesbian* various kinds of love letters between women—without "justification" other than to assert that lesbian is a way of loving and living for love. To be lesbian is simply to enjoy and suffer the dramatic experience of loving another, non-kin related, woman, of casting one's fate and future with her for however long. Virginia Woolf perhaps best captured the central feature of lesbian desire when she said, "Women alone stirred my imagination." I count all such passionate, imaginative, devoted love between women as lesbian.

There are lesbian moments and lesbian lifetimes. They can be discovered between new lovers and between dykes married for thirty years; among teenagers and octogenarians; in affectional, but non-sexual "Boston marriages"; and in the enduring relationships of couples who regularly practice their consenting version of S/M. Lesbian love is celebrated among women of all classes and knows no racial or religious determination. Love, the deepest form of human contact, is always possible——has always been possible——and often manifest between two women. Lesbian is a true feeling, a true way of being and no matter who has felt it, lived it, or denied it, lesbian exists as a knowledge and practice of the way one woman is given in love to and received by another.

This collection takes in a fairly broad sweep of *her*story; the earliest letter is dated 1852, the latest 1995. My project is based in the period since letter-writing became widespread and cheaply available to all——Britain had a penny post by 1840 and the five cent post was introduced in the United States in 1847. The modern Western epistolary tradition actually began in Europe in the 17th century. It was fueled by correspondence between privileged women of the courts and salons, but evidence of personal, even amorous

14

correspondence between women is found much earlier. The gay historian, John Boswell, discovered and translated a medieval missive addressed by one religious woman to another, in which she says, "When I recall the kisses you gave me, And how with tender words you caressed my little breasts, I want to die Because I cannot see you..."[3]

It is important to frame lesbian letter-writing within the larger tradition of women's correspondence, which in turn is linked to the general history of women's constraint under patriarchy. Letter-writing has for centuries been trivialized as a "woman's art." But this very trivialization led to the creation of a subversive genre. Letter-writing became a site of self-invention for women; on the page they expressed a version of the self in excess of what was considered appropriately "female" in a male world. What Shari Benstock explains in her discussion of the epistolary novel (written in letter-form or a novel that features letters) can be applied as well, I think, to the tradition of actual correspondence between women: "Letters provide freedom from the claims of reality precisely because they are private, recording desires necessarily silenced by prevalent social codes. Letters promise to reveal secrets, examine private passions, strip away the social mask, and expose the real person. They attempt to create an image of self and are the effect of such an effort."[4]

Women of an earlier age lived in letters and the passion of self-revelation they bestowed on each other in hours given to correspondence created a world both apart from and critical of the "real" world. Moreover, many of these women loved each other immensely, totally. For example, the early

19th-century correspondence between Mme de Staël and Mme Récamier is filled with ecstatic claims. Repeatedly, de Staël wrote to her confidante, "I love you with a love surpassing friendship." And in a letter of 1809 she summarized the political urgency binding their relationship, saying, "You have made me know all that is really sweet about love for a woman—it is the alliance of two weak creatures who face their oppressors together." By the mid-19th century, an emergent middle class in Europe and the U.S. produced a proliferation of passionate, self-determining letter-writing between women. From this point forward to the present, roughly the period represented here, enough letters exist to trace in them the trajectory of modern lesbian love and identity.

Carroll Smith-Rosenberg and Lillian Faderman's scholarship, which I have drawn on, is incomparable in establishing a sense of the female world of the 19th century. The social norms of that era did not proscribe intense, devoted relationships between women. As in centuries preceding it, the world was much more gender-divided than it is now. Women—mothers and daughters, sisters, cousins, and friends, both adolescent and adult—spent most of their time with each other and developed emotionally together. If they were separated—usually by marriage—devoted correspondence kept their emotional relations strong and dependent as well as providing a place for the expression of the woman-centered self. Within this context, Smith-Rosenberg suggests a spectrum of "emotional and sexual impulses" evolved to allow a wide latitude of psychosexual feelings. Letters of the period include many examples of what I would call lesbian. For example, a letter quoted by Smith-Rosenberg from Molly to Helena summarizes time they spent together this way: "Those two or three days so dark without, so bright with firelight and contentment within I shall always remember as proof that, for a time, at least—I fancy for quite a long time—we might be sufficient for each other.... I shall return in a few days. Imagine yourself kissed many times by one who loved you so dearly."[5]

Toward the end of the century, economic and political changes brought increasing independence to women, and perhaps not coincidentally, Faderman suggests, male sexologists' invention of the term "lesbian" to describe the "problem" of women's love for and sufficiency with each other.

Still, at the turn of the century the passionate partnerships of women such as Mary Woolley and Jeannette Marks, Amy Lowell and Ada Russell, and Jane Heap and Margaret Anderson, to name very few, were ongoing and relatively unquestioned, and a significant number of letters from the period openly claims an assertive sexual urge: "Just before you sink into slumber, dear heart, I rest in your arms. I browse amongst the roots of your hair—I kiss your body with biting kisses—I inhale the sweet, pungent odor of you and you plead with me for relief." (Almeda to Emma, c. 1912.)

Unfortunately, by the time "lesbian" became a more popular designation in the 1920s, it was used primarily as a label describing social-sexual abnormality and psychological "inversion." The demonization of lesbian desire became such that now language in the letters tended toward the cryptic: "You know I feel terribly much the way you do about it all, but I never could say so, even in incoherent fashion..." (Alice to Eleanor, c. 1920.) Women of this era were made miserable by the assumption of their difference as abnormal. Radclyffe Hall was often given to feelings of worthlessness and in 1934 complained bitterly to her mistress of suffering "the melancholy of the inverted." During the 1940s, lesbian lovers carried on devotedly, if discreetly, and many letters exist to prove it. But the next decade saw an era of repression and such fear that many lesbians destroyed the primary evidence of their love. Much to her current regret, Mildred Munday, a 77-year-old lesbian activist I spoke with in Ohio, burned all of her love letters in the late 1950s.

Thankfully, a major cultural and political shift was in the air by the early 1960s. A letter from 1961 exemplifies the turn from fear to fearlessness: "There must be something wrong with the world, I think. Why should we be afraid of what we feel, of what we think? Why should they be right, and we wrong?... It's not just a matter of a woman falling in love with another woman, it's a whole way of approaching life, a whole series of beliefs and ideals, and feelings, that is at stake. And I'm too selfish, too self-confident, to accept theirs instead of mine." (Charoula to Gail, 1961.)

After the subsequent rise of the Lesbian and Gay Liberation movements in the early 1970s, a change in the rhetoric of lesbian love is read in letters that openly proclaim the freedom of expressing a lesbian identity: "One day not too long ago I fell in love with a woman. I didn't try to or anything—it just happened. So now I am a Lesbian.... In spite of all the positive feelings growing within me, there is outrage sprouting. Seems that because I'm in love, there's pressure from the mainstream to become invisible. Well, I'm not invisible...." (Sue to Susan, 1975.)

Letters of the 1970s and early 1980s combine humorous depictions of pot-smoking and pussy-power and also deal with serious issues brought forward by the intersection of lesbianism and feminism: "I don't know when my strong body urges might be sexist rather than sexual—liberation has only confused me on this point and often I go through rather ridiculous self-debates over whether I'm sexual or sexist." (Karla to Anon, 1975.) The 1980s brought the "sex wars," a lively debate within lesbian circles continuing into the present, about the political and personal power of explicit sex practices. Current letters reflect the way love has been enhanced by an era open to new or previously repressed expressions of sexual passion. For example, the triumphant return of the dildo is recorded in Ann's letter to Gretchen of 1993: "This afternoon, maybe because we had talked and so reminded me of my body, I finally got around to masturbating for the first time since you left ... It was fun and part of what was exciting was that using the dildo (Blackie is associated in my mind and my body with being with you) ... I could feel like you were sort of there, maybe even that it was you fucking me, not me. So I guess that's an additional dividend of the dildo—those detachable body parts can stay at home to give me pleasure even when the rest of your body is off in another part of the country."

Other letters of the late 1980s and early 1990s recount the joys of S/M and a re-emergence of butch/femme identity, as well as a concern for love made public through marriage and permanent through children.

In the 20th century, the lesbian love letter has evolved from an intimate document of careful disclosure to a bold document of exuberant exposure. A full-length study of the material I collected would lend itself to much more detailed analysis than I can give in this discussion, but I want at least briefly to highlight some of the themes that unite my reading of these letters, both those found here and the many that could not be included in this volume. Certain of the themes might be found in any love correspondence: passionate outpourings, yearnings for reunion, jealousies, and so on. Other themes, I think, carry a characteristic lesbian sensibility about loving. I am not asserting here a theory of essential difference (nor have I drawn parallels with comparable heterosexual or gay male research material), yet I came to this project with a desire to understand further and promote the particular value of lesbian love as it has been shaped not only by history, but by choice. It is important to look at the letters as pure enactments of choice, of the way in which a woman ultimately unbridles convention and chooses to envision and express her love for another woman. The sense of a chosen intimacy—deeply compelling and hard won—is invested with a desire to inhabit a certain way of loving that affirms a unique intersection of the erotic and the ethical. Themes that appear and reappear in the letters articulate a feminine code of *entrustment* that includes choosing love for itself, not for what it will bring in terms of status; a commitment to a non-hierarchical, reciprocal relationship; alliance and friendship as part of loving; a strong desire for the beloved's personal self-fulfillment; honesty and respect as determining qualities of love; sex as the expression of intimacy; a feeling of trust, and a dedication to the effort required to express a precision of feeling.

This effort at precision drives the letters. We specify or we die, for in fact, as Elizabeth Meese suggests, the language exchanged between lesbian lovers invents the very possibility of being lesbian: "I make words, writing and more writing, to fill the lack and the imprecision ... with specification, to create variations on the possible through the shuttle of incalculable losses and gains as we translate each other, me to you, you to me. No one ever told me what my lesbian destiny could be, so I invent us."[6]

Perhaps this heightened need to "translate each other" explains why one of the most prevalent themes in lesbian love correspondence is the desire for letters, the waiting for letters, the immense joy in receiving letters, and the terrible disappointment when letters do not arrive. Over and over again the physical longing for letters is remarked in passages such as this one: "Well, when the wind opened the door, I saw the afternoon mail on the floor ... And my eagle eye at once detected a gray envelope ... Dear, do you know what it is to feel happy even at the sight of a 'stupid old gray envelope' (if it has the right handwriting on it?) ... I read that blessed letter more than once. I lay down an hour before dinner and took the letter with me, to read and reread. It was almost like seeing you ..."

(Mary to Jeannette, 1900.) And this more recent cry of relief: "I'm pleased to say that the desired effect of your fax was realized: a clitoral response ... And upon re-reading it, I'm happy to report, the sensation returned. The gift that keeps on giving." (Gretchen to Ann, 1991.) Such reported longing and fulfillment is connected to the universal way in which love letters serve as physical substitutes for the body of the beloved. But for lesbians the intensity of this longing is doubled in the sense that letters provide a necessary space not just for the expression but for the very creation and ratification of lesbian love. No wonder then that self-creation is at the very heart of lesbian loving. The lover is a mirror, each to each reflecting and validating feelings, dreams, and desires—a love based in similarity and connection as well as difference: "I awoke early this morning with a song in my heart and I have been awakening like this for four days now. I have never felt better physically or emotionally. It is YOU who has placed your hand inside my heart and plucked out its pain.... There are many things that I must write about. Your dreams, my dreams, our love, my sudden freedom inside me—both masculine and feminine—everything! Many minor miracles have occurred through your letters this week. I receive a letter from you and the night before or that very day I have expressed the parallel emotion...." (Bunny to Sandy, 1962.)

Along the same lines, in a recent letter a lover is prized as "a trustworthy mirror for the self-love I've painstakingly practiced ..." (Kay to Pat, 1994.)

Lesbian love is a source of freedom for the full exploration of the self. Mirroring is not about imitating; it is about uncensored narcissistic well-being and the possibility of self-determination supported by an Other who is also the Same: "We continuously amaze me ... We are always changing and growing. I appreciate how you support my growth. Offering me so many freedoms, so many paths towards self-growth. Watching you encourages me to grow for myself." (Charlene to Lori, 1993.)

Growth and change in the lesbian love relationship are propeled by fierce honesty and respect: "There is nothing to lose with honesty; there is everything to lose with unconsciousness." (Joanne to Brad, 1988.) Driven by a desire for honesty, the ethical dimensions of lesbian love are specified: "I love that we're nice to each other. I was thinking about that today. We are nice and respectful of each other—when we're alone or with other people. Do you feel the respect I have for you ... Do I treat you the way you want to be treated? Is my behavior consistent, whether alone or with others?... Do you feel how deeply I respond to you? I hope you do, and if you don't, that you would tell me. I don't feel that there's anything I haven't told you that I've needed to. I have been as honest as I know how ..." (Rebecca to Cherese, 1992.)

Honesty, the desire for disclosure, finds its physical expression in sexual love. The profound attachment women feel for each other is written through their letters on to the body of the beloved and specified there in details that combine intense erotic pleasure with a deeply felt intimacy, a need for innermost closeness: "Tiny Heart, I wish I could be near you tonight. Close, close—or near enough so that a look or touch would let either into the other's heart—or to feel the heart stagger under the added load of a kiss ..." (Jane to Florence, 1908.) Letters attempt to repair an absence that is both physical and emotional but they can also be a means of remembering the details of desire, using words to evoke the complexity of elements that combine to create love between women: "Thank you thank you thank you for your knowing hands and your wide mind and your honesty and your gentleness and your courage and your breasts and your hunger and your reading of Rumi and your fierce moments and your belly and your clear and shaded eyes and your sadnesses and your letting go and your listening and your face which changes and changes and your yearning and your yesses and your moments of bossiness and your yieldings and openings and opening wider and taking me in." (Anna to Rosie, 1993.)

The language of lesbian desire can be hot, purely sexual as in May Swenson's lusty, playful come-on, "I can't give you anything but sex baby/Can't offer you a penthouse or duplex baby/Just a cave in the wave where we can spoon/honey cake that we'll bake—and put lots of cream on baby." (May to Zan, 1967.) But at the core of lesbian sexuality is this desire for intimacy, the desire to be fully known at the innermost center of one's bodily, emotional, and spiritual being: "I want to send you to wondrous places so you can come back & tell me about them & we can try to figure out what the deal is about this thing called sex. And you. Your body. And me. My body.

And our hearts. Where & why does the heart connect w/the *vag*? What is it for me to love you?" (Gretchen to Ann, 1991.)

For the lesbian, the vagina is a direct route to the heart. Sex and emotion serve each other in the erotics of mutuality. As Gretchen later expresses it in the same letter, "Someday I want to do it. Really give myself to you w/all the passion I feel. Shoot you full of it, fuck you with my feelings." What in the past was expressed primarily through the rhetoric of yearning and kissing—"I hold you close my precious darling—Listen—can you hear me say I love you—and can you feel a long long kiss? I can!" (Margaret to Louise, 1913)—has become in the late 20th century the full-on rhetoric of fucking. Yet they create a continuum defining the complete desire for interjoining the physical, emotional, and spiritual dimensions of lesbian loving.

Of course relationships do end, but break-up letters continue to reveal the particular quality of lesbian loving. Some break-up letters dramatically disavow—"I hope you hurt a lot. I hope losing me puts a big black hole in your life. Right now I really hate you." (Paula to Jill, 1995), but others demonstrate a conscious attempt to express pain, regret, and separation as a first order for transforming passion into friendship: "I don't like saying 'no.' I'm not very good at it. Especially at the risk of you hating me, not understanding or believing my feelings for you (which are genuine, but not sexual). But no … I do not want to be your lover. I cannot be lovers with you. I will not act dishonestly, by doing something for you, to you, to 'make you feel better.' I'm sure you're aware of that deliberating voice within me that tosses back and forth, 'couldn't we just try again, couldn't I just do it right, couldn't I try being touched ... But ... I simply cannot risk acting out of obligation or pressure, or as a response to *your* needs. I am so sorry ... '" (Onzy to Rima, 1986.)

In the end, many of the correspondences I followed, including Onzy and Rima's, evolved from passionate, physical love to enduring friendship. Letter-writing records and often brings to effect the emotional work necessary to make this transition viable: "I wish you unconditional caring and support while getting involved with Erica ... All my love and gentleness is with you now, dear Kermie. Get some professional help to catalyze and advance this process of re-birthing yourself so you can get free of us to love fully—and live fully—again.... I want you to have someone to love and care for you and hold you when things go bump in the night...." (Mary Jo to Carol, 1983.) Lesbian love often doesn't finish; it regularly transforms demised couples into supportive family and community networks. Long after their romance ended, Vita Sackville-West wrote to Violet Trefusis in 1950: "I think we have got something indestructible between us ... a bond of child-hood and subsequent passion ... a very strange relationship, ours ... but unique in its way, and infinitely precious to me and (may I say?) to you...."

The letters gathered here touch upon these themes and others, but the pleasure of reading lesbian love letters is also found in simply enjoying the style and feel of the language women choose—the unself-conscious brilliance, the mundane pathos—in inimitably telling *écriture feminine*, a term espoused by the feminist French writer Hélène Cixous. Lesbian lovers have made the moon a metaphoric beacon for declaring female-centered passion: "Shall I ever stand in the moonlight without seeing and feeling beside me the white sweet flower of my perfect bride—my pure bride." (Margaret to Louise, 1913.) The moon, so richly symbolic of the feminine, is a source of comfort and inspiration to the lesbian lover. Calling upon the moon draws near someone who is far away: "Tonight is such a beautiful night Elsa—clear blue sky—stars like brilliant diamonds and a full moon. Often ... I stand looking out ... when the moon is shining—wondering if it was a clear night with you and maybe you could see the moon from your windows too or perhaps you might—even have stepped outside to gaze up at it in all its beauty." (Isabel to Elsa, 1947.)

The love of household cats—my preferred lesbian cliché—is remarked with great tenderness and humor. For example, Djuna Barnes's lover Thelma Wood writes gleefully about Dilly, even playfully scolding him for not writing: "Junie angel—Such a sweet letter from you—but Dilly he no write he pappa. When I get back—he will get a good birching...." (Thelma to Djuna, c. 1922.) Elsa Gidlow's lover "Tommy," writing to Gidlow during her extended stay in Europe during the late 1920s, always gave detailed accounts of their cats' health and daily activities: "The pussies send their love—they are sleeping off supper, on separate couches, after a lavish display of affection that seriously interfered with the writing of this letter ... Pierrot's pads are printed faintly on this sheet! He is ... now sitting on it, purring." (c. 1928.)

When I first realized that cats were a recurrent trope in the letters, I almost wondered if talking about pussies wasn't some kind of code for discussing *the* pussy. This theory did not pan out. In fact, cat-talk is actually a sign of domesticity, a figure of family that symbolizes the deepest connection between two women: "Darling, most beloved sister, how many cats have we had together? And some of them with our aching hands put to rest in blackest earth, as bottomless and fragrant as our eternally revolving lovers' bed ... where all of us still live." (Gail to Charoula, 1978.)

If cats can function at the spiritual level to symbolize the meaning of lesbian love, it is no wonder that traditional religious metaphors operate significantly to underscore the high value placed on relationships between women. Writing to Jeannette Marks in 1900, Mary Woolley pronounces that, "God in His Providence has given me this love when I most need it." And in another instance she, a Biblical scholar by academic training, rephrases the Old Testament passage remarking Jonathan's devotion to David—"Thy love to me was wonderful, passing the love of women"—saying to Jeannette, "Thy love to me *is* wonderful, passing the love of *men*" (my emphasis). One might expect God's Providence to play some role in condoning lesbian love at the turn of the century, but just as often a heretical impulse informs the rhetoric of lesbian love; a challenge to God and patriarchal convention extinguishes the niceties of "normalcy" in favor of sapphic ecstasy. Upon returning from church, Emily Dickinson writes to her beloved: "when he said 'Our Heavenly Father,' I said 'Oh Darling Sue'; when he read the 100th Psalm, I kept saying your precious letter all over to myself, and Susie, when they sang—it would have made you laugh to hear one little voice, piping to the departed. I made up words and kept singing how I loved you, and you had gone, while all the rest of the choir were singing Hallelujahs. I presume nobody heard me, because I sang *so small*, but it was a kind of comfort to think I might put them out, singing of you." (Emily to Susan, 1852.) This bit of blasphemy finds its complement over a century later in a letter dated 1994: "Through my baptismal Catholicism this year I am to sacrifice, in place of sweets or cigarettes, my lack of intimacy towards you.... As I kneel, how divine my suffering for this our first kiss on Ash Wednesday.... I care not if Easter comes." (Dana to Celeste.)

Religious metaphors are not always used to parody and subvert. In the past twenty years the feminist reclaiming of the Goddess has given a female-centered deity the task of symbolically guiding lesbian unions: "We need to ask some hard questions and take some hard steps—both of us do and that's for sure. But I pray that we can learn to take these steps while still keeping our faces and souls tuned and turned to the goodness between us and the Goddess." (Joanna to Margie, 1980.) Perhaps it can simply be said that for lesbians language itself has been our religion. Where we have freely expressed our love, letters are the common little bibles that bring us to believe in each other.

Finally, a necessary word about the editing and organization of this book. After reading thousands of letters, I narrowed my collection of about 600 letters down to 300, from which I chose those included here. The book is presented as a sampler; it is organized for variety and flow, rather than chronology. Collage illustrations were created by Sheri Tornatore and me (with additions from several other artist friends) as visual entertainment to accompany the reading. The collages were not usually made for particular letters, although in the end each one found a place with a letter that seemed right. To demonstrate as much variety as possible in a limited space, I elected to publish singular examples—that is, no correspondence between couples. Living letter-writers were allowed the opportunity to correct spelling and grammar as they wished, but an attempt was made to preserve the grammatical spirit of the original. Archived or previously published material of deceased writers was not corrected. A number of pieces were edited for length and deletions are indicated with ellipses.

As a way of continuing this project, I encourage lesbians everywhere to donate personal papers to local and national archives. Our gay and lesbian archives currently contain excellent materials on the public aspects of lesbian and gay history and liberation. We have a wonderful and accessible record of posters, buttons, pamphlets, magazines, journals, and books. But most archives contain little of the intimate, personal materials—the evidence of lesbian and gay love which gave rise to our desire for liberation in the first place. Letters are crucial manifestoes of our loving. At the center of lesbian freedom in the world is the inviolable love of one woman for another written down in a letter.

30

NOTES

1. Anne Carson, *Eros: The Bittersweet* (Princeton: Princeton University Press, 1986) 98–99.
2. Judy Grahn, *The Highest Apple: Sappho and the Lesbian Poetic Tradition* (San Francisco: Spinsters Ink, 1985): 75.
3. John Boswell, *Christianity, Social Tolerance, and Homosexuality: Gay People in Western Europe from the Beginning of the Christian Era to the 14th Century* (Chicago and London: University of Chicago Press, 1980): 220–221.
4. Shari Benstock, *Textualizing the Feminine: On the Limits of Genre* (Norman and London: The University of Oklahoma Press, 1991): 91–92.
5. This letter, written c. 1869–70, is in the Mary Hallock Foote Letters collection, Stanford University, and was included in Carroll Smith-Rosenberg, "The Female World of Love and Ritual: Relations Between Women in Nineteenth-Century America," *Signs: Journal of Women in Culture and Society* (University of Chicago. Vol. I, No. I, fall 1975, pp. 1–29): 6.
6. Elizabeth Meese, *(Sem)erotics* (New York: New York University Press, 1992): 127–128.

FURTHER READING

Barthes, Roland. *A Lover's Discourse: Fragments.* Translated by Richard Howard. New York: Hill and Wang, 1978. London: Jonathan Cape, 1979.

Bishop, Elizabeth. *One Art: Letters.* Selected and edited by Robert Giroux. New York: Farrar, Straus & Giroux, 1994.

Carson, Rachel. *Always, Rachel: The Letters of Rachel Carson and Dorothy Freeman, 1952–1964.* Edited by Martha Freeman. Boston: Beacon Press, 1995.

Carter, Elizabeth. *Letters from Mrs. Elizabeth Carter to Mrs. Montagu Between the Years 1755–1800.* Edited by Montagu Pennington. 3 Vols. London: E.C. and J. Rivington, 1817.

Cherewatuk, Karen and Ulrike Wiethaus (eds.). *Dear Sister: Medieval Women and the Epistolary Genre.* Philadelphia: The University of Pennsylvania Press, 1993.

Dickinson, Emily. *The Letters of Emily Dickinson.* Edited by Thomas H. Johnson and Theodora Ward. 3 Vols. Cambridge, MA: Harvard University Press, 1958.

Faderman, Lillian. *Surpassing the Love of Men: Romantic Friendship and Love Between Women from the Renaissance to the Present.* New York: William Morrow and Co., 1981. London: The Women's Press, 1981.

———. *Odd Girls and Twilight Lovers: A History of Lesbian Life in the Twentieth*

Century. New York: Columbia University Press, 1991. London: Penguin, 1992.

————. *Chloe Plus Olivia: An Anthology of Lesbian Literature from the Seventeenth Century to the Present.* New York: Viking Penguin, 1994.

Flanner, Janet. *Darlinghissima: Letters to a Friend.* Edited and with a commentary by Natalia Danesi Murray. New York: Harcourt Brace Jovanovich, 1985. London: Pandora, 1988.

Gidlow, Elsa. *I Come with My Songs: The Autobiography of Elsa Gidlow.* San Francisco: Booklegger Publishing, 1986.

Hanscombe, Gillian and Virginia L. Smyers. *Writing for Their Lives: The Modernist Women: 1910–1940.* London: The Women's Press, 1987.

Katz, Jonathan. *Gay American History.* New York: T.Y. Crowell Co., 1976.

Kauffman, Janet. *Discourses of Desire: Gender, Genre, and Epistolary Fiction.* Ithaca, N.Y., and London: Cornell University Press, 1986.

Levaillant, Maurice. *The Passionate Exiles: Madame de Staël and Madame Récamier.* New York: Farrar, Straus and Cudahy, 1958.

O'Brien, Sharon. *Willa Cather: The Emerging Voice.* New York and London: Oxford University Press, 1987.

Orne Jewett, Sarah. *Letters of Sarah Orne Jewett.* Edited by Annie Fields. Boston: Houghton Mifflin, 1911.

Sackville-West, Vita. *The Letters of Vita Sackville-West to Virginia Woolf.* Edited by Louise DeSalvo and Mitchell A. Leaska. New York: Morrow, 1985. London: Hutchinson, 1984.

Sappho. *Sappho and the Greek Lyric Poets.* Translated by Willis Barnstone. New York: Schocken Books, 1988.

Smith, Lillian. *How Am I to Be Heard? Letters of Lillian Smith.* Edited by Margaret Rose Gladney. Chapel Hill and London: University of North Carolina Press, 1993.

Todd, Janet. *Women's Friendship in Literature.* New York: Columbia University Press, 1980.

Trautmann, Joanne. *The Jessamy Brides: The Friendship of Virginia Woolf and V. Sackville-West.* University Park: Pennsylvania State University, 1973.

Trefusis, Violet. *Violet to Vita: The Letters of Violet Trefusis to Vita Sackville-West.* Edited by Mitchel A. Leaska and John Phillips. New York and London: Penguin, 1991.

Woolf, Virginia. *The Letters of Virginia Woolf.* Vol. 3, 1923–1928. Edited by Nigel Nicholson and Joanne Trautmann. London: Hogarth Press, 1975. New York: Harcourt Brace Jovanovich, 1977.

THE LETTERS

Dear L,

How should I address you in my love letters? L, my lesbian(ism), my Lover, my love, through the glistening pip, the shining tendril (of) your desire for me, the slender rod registering the relation of your frequency and mine. My task is to convert you and me to us. You are you. I want you to be separate so that I can feel the thrill of taking (you) over, composing you/me/ mine/ours. For a moment I construct you/me: inseparable, just as I write the word "us" or we — a rewriting of you/me. A momentary substitution. The "you" standing in for you is the machinery that makes these letters possible. Overdrive: overwrite. What is passion without the dream of a resistance, a difference even ever so slight, to be overcome as I push you down on the bed, a distance to be bridged as I cover your body with mine, I orchestrate and perform my desire on your smooth skin, I play the fuck master and take you (in). Perhaps there is not even a sound.

Love,

L

So sweet and still, and Thee, Oh Susie, what need I more, to make my heaven whole?

Sweet Hour, blessed Hour, to carry me to you, and to bring you back to me, long enough to snatch one kiss, and whisper Good bye, again.

I have thought of it all day, Susie, and I fear of but little else, and when I was gone to meeting it filled my mind so full, I could not find a <u>chink</u> to put the worthy pastor; when he said "Our Heavenly Father," I said "Oh Darling Sue"; when he read the 100th Psalm, I kept saying your precious letter all over to myself, and Susie, when they sang—it would have made you laugh to hear one little voice, piping to the departed. I made up words and kept singing how I loved you, and you had gone, while all the rest of the choir were singing Hallelujahs. I presume nobody heard me, because I sang so <u>small</u>, but it was a kind of comfort to think I might put them out, singing of you. I a'nt there this afternoon, tho', because I

36

am here, writing a little letter to my dear Sue, and I am
very happy. I think of ten weeks — Dear One, and I think

of love, and you, and my heart
grows full and warm, and my
breath stands still. The sun
does'nt shine at all, but I can
feel a sunshine stealing into
my soul and making it all
summer, and every thorn, a
<u>rose</u>. And I pray that such
summer's sun shine on my
Absent One, and cause her
bird to sing!

You have been happy,
Susie, and now are sad — and
the whole world seems lone;
but it wont be so always,
"some days <u>must</u> be dark and

dreary"! You wont cry any more, will you, Susie, for my
father will be your father, and my home will be your
home, and where you go, I will go, and we will lie side by
side in the kirkyard. . . .

Emilie —

Dearest Elsa—

Every night when I go to bed I write an imaginary letter to you—little happenings of the day—thoughts born of a passage of music heard or a line of poetry—so often I would like to put them down on paper but were I to do so, your mail would become burdensome & with nothing more than my dreamy ramblings dear. . . .

This is your Christmas letter—to wish you so much happiness Elsa & though I cannot be beside you to see you burn the Christmas pudding . . . the corner of my heart that holds my thoughts of you will travel the many miles that separate us so that once again you will feel me near you. As I light the Christmas Candle at dusk on Christmas Eve, Elsa, a little bit of me will start out—to you dear.

The Holidays should be a time of pleasant memories— & I am wondering if you remember the Christmas Candles in the villages in England? It is one of my earliest remembrances. . . . as a very little girl I was allowed to light the Candle that was placed in the window with the curtains drawn far back, to light the Christ Child into the world, & regardless of religious beliefs or disbeliefs, I think it is such a beautiful custom that I still adhere to . . . .

*Those are years gone by—it is to-day that matters &
into my "to-day"—unwittingly perhaps on your part—
you have come. . . . No Elsa—I don't change like April.
. . . there is a way to, if one is sincere & if it is really so,
to make the other person feel or rather know that you are
theirs completely. Since receiving your letter I have
thought a lot about it & wondered if I was wrong in
thinking the way I do. I realize it is a definite hang-over
from my married years when I was absolutely
puritanical—The—how shall I put it? The transition
was after my husband died—& why—I will never
understand, though from books I have read, there must
have been a tendency even if only subconsciously. It
worried me for years—When you hear (because I will not
write it) that chapter I don't think you are going to
want to believe me, but Elsa every word will be true. . . .*

*Now the hands on the clock are allmost at 2A.M. . . .
Where was I before I digressed so far? Back to you dear
& the joy it has given me to know you even though it be
but through the medium of letters. . . .*

So "Happy Christmas" to Lao & you dear
My love—

Isabel

Dear Love,
I'm biding my time in Brooklyn.
This is the in-between time of
magic and hot coffee. Every time
I think I've made my bed it stays
lonely and wondering. With
friends like these who needs sleep?
I thought the center of this
journey would appear with bright
lights and celestial horns but it
appears to be the flames on my
spine winning our attention.
I'm developing my smoking skills
and my pace has slowed to a
fevered pitch. The neighbors are
beginning to notice. "How long is
she staying?" whispered the
woman in apartment 4. "You
girls should get some sleep."
Write when you can,

Your love

Dear Heart — my own —

Your little letter sounded just like Tommy's little bird that was so glad for the sunshine, that he broke his little heart singing. After all wasn't he a foolish little bird — who was the sunshine made for if not for him? My dear dear Tiny Heart, why shouldn't you have all the love that Hattie and I can give you? And don't get frightened over the little we can express — Think of the vast unsaid. I have always felt that I was a good lover; but since I have loved you I feel how utterly impossible it is to convey an idea of my love to you. Except, perhaps by some symbol of beauty, of which great love is a part, it is nearly impossible. If I ever write a "pome" or paint a picture that approaches the absolute beauty then you may see my love for you.

I thank you for entrusting your sister's letter to me. . . . I am glad you mean to her and her child what she feels you do. You know the little sentiment I have in regard to your mother. I always have tenderness and a feeling of pity for her — because you are not really hers.

It seems as if her love for you and her fear of losing you had made a bond between us. It seems to me that all

42

the Gods are enemies, I trust none. Oh if I should have to lose you! I feel such hate at the very thot that I could crush the earth and pull down the heavens and destroy the little and big Gods — (I wonder what first barbaric lover felt thusly?).

Now you two are to see one another . . . Maybe you can tell her a little of our love? I should like to see her. I know I should like her. And she would like me. No Fear! . . .

I have been thinking very much these days of Beauty— (poor name is it not for anything so Holy). I know that if everyone felt Beauty strongly, felt that everything beautiful was God and all things not beautiful not God. That woman was the nearest symbol for Beauty. If one could see this—there would be no sin, or squalor, or unhappiness in the whole world.

I wonder what you do these beautiful starry nights. I long for you, to sit with me and watch them—to see if they were sneering at our little day and helplessness—or whether in their impotent aloofness they do not long for even a little Human love. And would exchange all their calm bright coldness for one warm young kiss. . . .

Dear little wind-bell voice I pine to hear you. Good night, Loved So Well, I wish you were here tonight and every night to go to sleep on my arm.

Your Jane

To the Amazon:
Joan dear:

Your letters arrive slowly—I hunger for more always. The distance, not the climate, is cruel. With your letters before me, I can hear the lifting tones of your voice, its clarity and rounded edges. I can feel the breath of your speech as I move from line to line. The sensation of you caught on those pages relieves the ache of your absence.

Today, I would like to talk about the fish here. Buried deep beneath the ice caps are a beautiful little-known species of pike. To catch them is an art—much like a writer casting about for words to reveal the soul and heart to the lover. Lately, I have been going out fishing with Najo, a native of these parts. We cut a hole in the ice with powered auger—not the nostalgic saw many envision. Najo flips a perfect circle of ice, thick and frosty, onto the surface nearby with her tonged pole like a large white discus hurled from a giant shoulder. It skids to a stop. We set up an ice house to protect us from the bitter winds.

Slicing the bait comes first, a squid. Odd to sacrifice one sea creature for another. Now wrapped with the long slices of rubbery flesh, the hooks slowly sink by measure into the icy water—lower and lower. Here in the Arctic the water doesn't cool with depth but rather it warms. (I think of you stretched out under me, likewise hotter at the center, and I flush.)

The time that follows exists on its own plane, a restful anticipation.

This day I remember brought a rainbow catch—the fish were markers of the northern lights. They glowed beneath the surface and above. I recall our expedition in Wellfleet when you tossed the fish you caught back—a game of catch with the sea. A feared formula of retribution you later confided, a family of correspondence that recalls a death, however small, in the hereafter.

But it is life that fills me. Your arrival squarely at my center has changed me. May Swenson often writes of "luck" in her poems—a way that life can have of comfortably enjoying, not solving, its mysteries. Luck is a synchronic click with the natural that takes you above dilemma and quite simply provides. To be lucky is to

possess a key in this life—to inhabit a sphere of understanding. Love is luck—I believe—and you, Joan, have taught me that.

It is you I catch here, Joan, the light and the luck of you.

Dearest A.,

I keep thinking about what you said about wanting us to raise the child together. If you're serious, there's nothing I'd like more. A flood of images come: turning to you in the truck over the sleeping head of the child; looking up from nursing him/her as you come in at the end of a long day . . . the first words, the first tottery steps; both of us watching as a sturdy two-year-old races around a garden: the flowers, the sunlight, our mutual joy (and exhaustion!). Of course I want this if you do. I want your intelligence and warmth and focus and commitment. I want your old crow's laugh. I want the sense of being known by you . . . which, in the whelm and flux of motherhood, would be especially precious. <u>But</u>—

If you do not really want these things, if you're only saying you do because you want me and right now I'm a madonna on the rocks, I come "with child," then you need to be extremely careful. We could set ourselves up for the worst time of our lives . . . if you said yes to this parents' lark and didn't mean it . . . A child eats up time and money and attention. Not much writing gets done . . . Not much love gets made (at least, if love means sex). "I don't want to have a child," you said to me long ago. "Because

48

most mothers are servants, and I don't want to be a servant." . . .

The more deeply I surrender to my longing to be your lover, your life partner, your spouse,* the more I feel obligated to be honest about the rocky places between us. There are the old rocks of competition and resentment: competition over friends and ownership of friends, competition over writing and skill and success and opportunity. There is resentment, deep corroding resentment, about love and generosity: what's "enough" and what isn't. These things have been laid aside (dissolved?) in the fervor of our love-making, but that doesn't mean they don't exist. . . .

So what it comes down to, darling Stevenson, is please look out for yourself. *I can't do this work for you*. If you trick yourself into thinking you want marriage and a child when you really don't, all three of us will suffer. . . . I want you, of course I do. But I don't want a surly, grudging, guilty partner. I don't want someone who would rather be elsewhere: out in the garden, back at the desk. You can be an interested aunt *anyway*, you know. I love you and will welcome you in whatever role you choose. (This is true. Don't forget it.) All my love as always,

Rosie XXX

* I like that on paper anyway, *spouse* rhymes with *house* and of course *mouse*. Does that mean that the plural of spouse is *spice*? Now there's a lively notion!

March 24, 1994

Dear Joan,

If I were to die before I got to tell you this in person, (hopefully later today), I couldn't rest easy for a long time.

There is a much longer version, but I'll cut to the chase: Any moron with enough time and enough lubrication could make me come rubbing my clit. Only Joan can get me this aroused and this contented by rubbing my feet.

This is the real thing.

See you soon.

Love,

M.E.

Dearest Marla—

I just came home, sat down on the edge of my bed and, as I bent down to untie my shoes (still wearing those bad-boy, fence-banging Oxfords), I burst into tears. I knew the crying meant it is time to write to you, that, of all the projects I am procrastinating about (most for reasons mysterious to me, just that shadow that falls between the intention and the action . . .), this letter to you is the one that can't be postponed any longer. I don't know what it is about tying or untying my shoes—probably it was my first autonomous act, and so my whole early childhood is imprinted in the gesture—but I have more than this once begun sobbing even before I get the double-knot (the just-in-case knot ...) untied.

Actually, I didn't mean to start this letter off by mentioning the middle "P" in the three P's of Perfectionism> Procrastination> Paralysis (a handy and all too relevant slogan I picked up somewhere), meant instead to write you a positive perky pal-sy . . . letter this time, finally a newsy normal note (sorry about this alliterative tic—I guess I'm trying to lighten up, get over myself, & show both me & you that I am not pathologically serious, have made much progress out of the heartbreak hotel I've lived in since you left me), all about what I have been doing, not about what I have not been doing . . .

Expressing how I feel is a major impetus behind this letter, too. This is not new news: I still love you. I would be lovers with you again in a hot millisecond, with no hesitation, as if this year & a half without you never happened, was just a scary dream. I have feelings & thoughts about you every day. I do not feel my devotion to you, to the memory of us together, is a sick obsession. It feels right to me. My continuing love for you is one of the purest feelings in my heart.

Today a small event happened that demonstrated for me how I am still being faithful to you. A young, strapping, boyish dyke with a huge clump of keys on the right (who I'd met shortly after you left and who intrigued me because she looked like a junior version of you) . . . offered herself to me today and, though I felt tempted, I held her at arms-length and graciously refused. I felt that my heart belongs to you and that sport-fucking (like using drugs, drinking, smoking) is a stimulant/escape I do not choose to take *today. What I am saying . . . is that I have been celibate since you & I last made love. There are several reasons for this: any potential sex partner looks totally two-dimensional to me compared to my multi-dimensional view of you; I have worked too hard to have a self, and some precious emotional sobriety, to risk losing it to sex/romance; I'm putting much of my sexual energy into developing a rich relationship with myself . . . and building healthy friendships with others; I have searched deep within my soul for a personal code of sexual ethics, have decided that sex is for me a sacred intimacy & not just a way to supercharge a dying ego or a way to get off, & until I happen into a situation that meets my criteria . . . I will remain celibate; I am scared to death of the pain I now associate with intimacy; plus other reasons I haven't named yet. . . .*

Well . . . "enough's enough, already," as my mother would say. I sure would love to get some details about your life: I hope you'll write me soon.

Love,

Rita

Thyme,

Stoned. Alone in Circle House, this enchanted place of shadows & vaulted height. It's magical with or without dancing women. It is a holy space, a presence. I am at peace . . .

Time for change. Thyme for change?

Maybe you hate those jokes. I figure you must be open to them, though; your name is intentional. I think it's wonderful, always have thought so. Bethroot, too, is an herb. Relieves female distress. Also, an aphrodisiac. Parent family of the trillium, the nightshade. Earth and ether.

Listen, I have to do it this way. I live an hour-plus away from the nearest dykes I know . . . I can't afford to play the cautious, testing games, the delicate dance of waiting until I happen to see you again; it could be months. . . . But in the meantime, I want to be clear: I enjoyed flirting with you at Halloween; I enjoyed singing with you at Halloween; I felt a nice charge between us; and I'd like to see you more. . . .

They say a comment here or there that leads me to sense difficulties often in your close-up personal life. I choose difficult people. I am a difficult person. . . . more difficult is often more interesting, yes? More substantial.

And I remember that you are a writer. A radio pioneer. I like that. Funny, to be adding stuff up about someone I know so barely. It just looks, senses right to me that you have turned up in my universe; I'd like to entertain our possibilities. . . . Whatever you say. I'm not going to bad trip myself for being direct. It feels refreshing to take responsibility for getting what I want. I want new connections, closeness with other women. . . .

This letter does not intend to be about arrangements & details. It wishes to tell you that I'm thinking of you & wondering whether it would please you for us to have a "date" (as they say in the vernacular). . . .

I have a lot of inner, psychic work to do. I am encouraged: this is my process, this being direct, is part of my work. Taking responsibility, not leaving initiative to the other, or to Fate. Shaping Fate. And being clear about contentment that is available inside myself no matter how things turn out. Learning happiness: karmic task.

Sure as the wind, my sister
And sure as the rain,
Sure as the sun does shine
We shall meet each other again . . .

Love, Bethroot

I look forward to
delivering this in person
Where do you
live?

Viva Sher Indica
and illumina fenix

I will mail
myself
if need be

Ann,

I feel so much for you. It just courses thru my body. Since I'm not calling it, categorizing it, defining it "being in love," it means I just have to feel it & feel it & feel it. . . . I'm filled w/all this emotion, all these fond recollections, all these imaginative plans, this constant desire to feel your fingers in me far, have you move me. God, it just comes rushing up. I think I might well have a <u>tremendous</u> desire for you. What a thing to feel . . . I want to be w/you. I want access to your person . . . You who move me in so many deep ways, new ones. God, I just want to fuck you for it. I want to fuck you for what you've given me . . . I want to send you to wondrous places so you can come back & tell me about them & we can try to figure out what the deal is about this thing called sex. And you. Your body. And me. My body. And our hearts. Where & why does the heart connect w/the <u>vag</u>? What is it for me to love you? . . . Why do I feel compelled to say it, to have you know? . . .

I'm a gushing girl. I could gush. I could not hold back. Could overwhelm you w/all this emotion you incite. . . . Someday I want to do it. Really give myself to you w/all the passion I feel. Shoot you full of it, fuck you w/my feelings. Make them crash over you like waves. . . . Oh,

Ann. Ann. I am full of you today. . . . Oh, I love you, Ann. I'm not going to be afraid to just write it, have it in print for you to see. I love you, Ann. I want to be your friend. So badly. I want to love you freely & well. I want you to know I care. . . . Dear God, this is a lot. Fuck me, Ann, make me know you. Make your presence known & undeniable. . . . Get inside me, do your work . . .

Always it seems to come back to the physical realm, fucking. That's such a powerful thing to do. And it's free. I love that part. . . . Let's go, Ann. Let's shoot off. I don't mind danger. I want to give it to you. That's that. I want to take from you. That's certain. . . .

Gretchen

Djuna love—I wrote you a letter last week but had sense enough to read it over the next day—and not send it. It was awful—I thought I was going to have a "crisis" but I was unwell and perhaps that was the trouble—

But at times Djuna things get very terrible—something will happen and I go to pieces—for instance I dream of you every night—and sometimes Djuna I dream we are lovers and I wake up the next day and nearly die of shame. Taking advantage in my sleep of something I know so intimately—and something you do not wish me to have—Its like stealing from you and I feel the next day like cabling "forgive me" and sitting up all night.

You can understand dearest how I get upset—have patience with me—your letter about knowing what I ought to do torments me. I say to myself "Djuna is a clever woman—and she must know how I tear myself up over every word she writes"—and if theres something to do its not what I've done or am—I'd cut my heart out and send it to you if you cared for it—I'd do anything in the world to please you a little—but what is it I can do? . . .

. . . I want you my Djuna—you know you have my life—in any way you want it—I'll be president of the United States if you want it—I adore you—

Simon

*. . . It is already wet there, where my hand reaches. I
imagine it is your hand, and through you I touch myself.
My body responds with the immediacy that comes from
wanting too long. You are one hour away by air, and I
can feel you . . . I slide my fingers in and around the
curves and folds of me, and draw my hand to my face so I
can smell and taste what you do to me . . . I can feel . . .
your mouth on me. Everywhere it brushes my skin I am
branded. The marks of you making me yours. With every
kiss, with every touch, I become more yours, until you are
deep inside me and I am no one's. I am unraveling,
dissipating into oblivion, becoming pieces in your mouth
for you to savor, to roll with your tongue and to hold
gently with your teeth. You are taking me there, where I
am lost, dislodged from the here and now of my existence.
I am coming, raging through a tunnel of darkness, then
light, delivered in your hands as shrapnel. You carefully
hold me in your folds while I reinvent myself with you.
. . . I want to move slowly; I want to know everything
about becoming.*

*I can feel your body, wanting. I fold my fingers
through yours and make a fist between you and me. It
is a pact, made of flesh and blood that is us and our*

desire. I . . . look on the power that is your body. I want to know it better than you.. . . I want to feel it teaching me about you. . . . I want my mouth on you . . . I . . . slowly push . . . you . . . open . . . This is the inspiration. Engorged with what is life and what is woman. I lower myself to you . . . I open my mouth and take you with my tongue . . . I have not known desire like this. It is maniacally demanding, non-negotiating, unyielding, intrusive. I want to push myself so deep inside of you that I disappear. . . . I pull out, and I push back in, slowly, again and again . . . The rhythm quickens . . . We are no longer human. We are somewhere outside ourselves

rushing toward a high thin sound, that is you coming all over me . . . in that crescendo of shudders and cries is my deliverance. I hold fast. I gather you. I keep you from harm. I kiss you . . . Your mouth breathes life in and out of both of us. . . .

HAPPY BIRTHDAY BEAUTIFUL . . . It's such a lovely day here, the goddesses know its your birthday and have made everything stunning for you. I thought I would honor your memory in my own way and I got up and took a long bath and put on my leather pants and red jacket and boots and red lipstick like the first time I caught your eye on the bar stool that night when I held your attention long enough to get you to my motel room, if even for a moment, but it was enough to light the flame, which has not quit burning burning burning since and I love it so much, you, how it happened, where it is going, how good we look together on the street and how well we fit together under covers or on top of them or next to each other on the subway and I think YES YES this is as fine as fine gets only for us it will only get better and better, a thought that is awesome in its own right, when I think of you and what is growing between us like marigolds or zinnias, fast and furious in bold colors springing up all over the place, between cracks in city sidewalks and beside front porch swings bringing something wonderful and beautiful to all of those who walk by or see or feel it, and it is good to see it pass along among friends who can recognize THE GOOD and feel it and it rubs off on them and courses thru their bones too, this wonderful wonderful love that has come like Venus up from the waters, cool and sweet it makes me want to take you now, right now in my arms and hold you and kiss you everywhere everywhere not missing a single spot and love you with my mouth and my hands and my arms and my face so good it feels next to you, so perfect you feel, so perfect we are together cracking whips and gum and so happy we are, I am, I am so happy to know you, so happy you were born today 29 years ago and so proud of your strength and your big brave heart baby that I just want to say from the bottom and top of my heart that I hope you have a happy day and a happy happy birthday and I love you so so much. . . .

Yours yours yours with love — Lu

Madisson, Madisson, Madisson,

I am obsessed with you. I can't eat. I can't sleep. I only can think of you & our love-making on Friday night. Thoughts of you crying—thinking of how beautiful I find you. Being scared to let me kiss you everywhere—afraid to let go of the last control to me—afraid to be so totally vulnerable. . . . I want to possess you, capture you, belong to you. Belong to you—belong to you—belong to you. Madisson, I belong to you. I surrender my body, my heart, my soul to you, my beautiful Madisson.

I am more afraid than I have ever been in my life. Afraid of the totality of my desire for you. Afraid you'll ask me to leave Terry, afraid you won't ask me to leave Terry. What's going to happen to me? . . . How can I live without you now that I've found you? I cannot. . . .

Come to my house on our next weekday off & spend the day with me. Start in the morning, make love, go on a picnic, hold hands, tell me your dreams, make love again & again & again. . . . Let me court you, woo you, seduce you. . . . Let me rub our wetness together. This time I won't hold back my climax. I love your hands, lips, pelvis, legs. . . . I love you, angel. I love you

*Janet Madisson Mary Michael Ledét forever & without
conditions or hesitation. If you reject me now—I will die.*

Laura

Dearest Ms. Cohen,

In response to your delightful request for more information regarding my LOVE & LUST LETTER WRITING WORKSHOPS, I thought I would give you a brief yet concise overview of my approach. Years of experience and research have led to the development of my program, which is designed to meet the needs of any lovesick individual with a special someone in mind.

Several factors need to be considered when thinking about entering the exciting and titillating world of LLLW. May I suggest that to begin, you sit in a circle with yourself, take a long deep breath, pause for a moment and ask yourself, "Am I in love and lust with anyone?" This is very critical, for if the answer is no, then there is no reason to proceed and you may now disregard the rest of this letter. But, if you are fortunate enough to answer YES, then let's go on.

Next, you need to find a pen, one that is comfortable in your hand, easy to use, of a color that will truly reflect your feelings of the moment (e.g., red for passion or blue for blue). Often times, an LLL receiver can become quite excited over a letter written in multi-colors but I recommend waiting to try the rainbow effect until you

have completed an advanced LLLW.

Now it's important to acquire just the right paper, card, or fax machine as the perfect medium to carry the illicit emotion behind the pen. Color is important here, as well, and texture can be significant also. After all, that special someone will be holding your letter instead of you. May I suggest a dab of your very own fragrance for that extra intimate touch.

We're ready now to just let those words appear on the page. Don't be shy. LOVE AND LUST LETTER WRITING is a perfect way to tend to a long distance relationship — very

much like caring for plants. They need water and sun and a little TLC in order to grow. Just let those tender, loving, gentle, passionate, sexy, mushy, inspiring, encouraging thoughts to your lustee reveal themselves on the page. The rewards can be phenomenal. Try to avoid using terms such as poopsy, lovey-dovey, and soulmate, although some clichés can be appropriate.

Lastly, find a stamp and envelope. It is most important to mail the LLL you have just so elegantly created. Forgetting this step can ruin the entire process.

Please feel free to practice with me at any time and I will be sure to respond. LOVE AND LUST LETTER WRITING is state-of-the-art for the 1990's. I wish you the best of luck and am sending you much encouragement to begin today.

Yours in LOVE AND LUST,

M.T. Silvia

. . . I am a savage, Emma, a wild, wild savage. And they can't tame me with their puling conventions, their stinking houses nor their damned religion. And it is the untamed part of me that loves you because you don't want to put leading strings on it. If you did I would tell you that you are a liar and your book is a lie.

And it is the wild part of me that would be unabashed in showing its love for you in front of a multitude or in a crowded room. My eyes would sparkle with love—they would follow you about and love to gaze upon you always and every part of my body would be replete with satisfaction of its express-ion of love.

God! God! God! God!

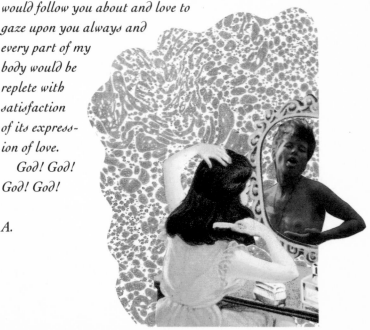

A.

Querida,

Are you really my querida? Must we wait for time to tell us everything? Or will we, like Faust, command the hours?

Whenever I'm depressed, as I am now (and angry that you're with Anna, and angry that I can't be more certain of myself or my needs), I sound like a low-rent philosopher . . . I realize that some sun would make a great difference in my life. I'm yearning to be naked in the summer sunlight . . .

I checked with friends in NY, and no one did anything at all for International Women's Day—it has vanished as a possibility here except for the middle-income, middle-brow MS Magazine set. The U.S. is the only major country that doesn't officially recognize our day. Ah, I long for those wonderful marches we used to have down Fifth Avenue with all women holding hands and still able to say nice things about each other!

My suggestion for International Women's Day is, as you know, to liberate all the maids in South America. Should I travel to Brazil on that slogan? I could dress up like my name-sake Jeanne d'Arc in elaborate armor and ride a white horse from favela to favela with a fluttering

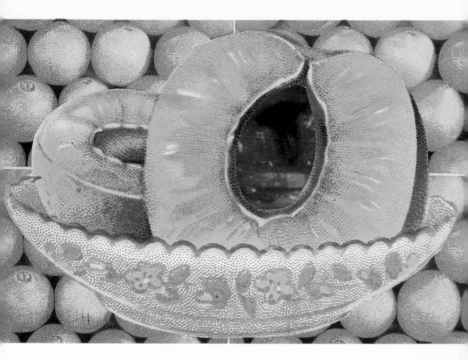

oriflamme (you need a very good English dictionary to find __that__ word) emblazoned with LIBERATE THE MAIDS. I wonder who would kill me first? The bourgeoisie—or the maids? . . .

. . . Remember, I said that it was easier for me to be alone, I didn't say it was desirable. . . . I'm thinking a lot about your beautiful __busceta__.

Love, sunlight, lots of warm kisses—Joan

Annette,

As you sleep, I am up walking around, sitting, standing, sitting again, strumming the guitar, looking around, overall, missing you.

I come across Alice Toklas . . . The memories of those women who love and love and live their life. . . .

I am struck by a thought. I never, never want to lose you . . . and I think of the things that "go without saying"

And I wonder why would anything go without saying?

So, I say that I love you, although you know it must take a lifetime to explain and it will.

That I will love you forever

That I will care for you . . .

That I will always respect you

That I am proud of you

That I will honor you

That I am your family and you are mine and we are of the world, to change it and change with it —

That when you are not with me for a few minutes, that even when you are asleep,

I want to show up in your dreams and kiss you forever.

Te amo, Dita.

April 29 1995

Dear Audrey,

You wonder why I did not tell you that I really love you. You wanted to hear the words so badly. But remember how I explained to you that . . . those words mean so little . . . when said too much, too soon, for too many reasons. I tell you I love you in so many ways. When I tell you how I love the fire inside you or the way you try to make people around you happy. Remember when I read that poem with you, "Diving Into the Wreck"? I wanted to show you real love by sharing something that means a lot to me. If you have ever experienced real love, you would never want an imitation. Imitation as in fake or pretend love, not the real thing. Just words . . .

Before we broke up, I felt oppressed at times. You wanted me to be with you all the time. I needed "air", or space as the diver in the poem needs to explore herself . . . The diver "goes down", deep indside herself to find her strength . . . Audrey, you are so strong inside. You came to this country even though English is not your first language and you are deaf. Still you communicate with people everyday. . . . You don't need someone to be with you always, to make you happy. Your happiness starts inside you, loving yourself. . . . I'm not saying that it is

76

an easy journey; the diver finds it difficult to move when she tries to change direction. . . . There are risks. I wish I could tell you that by accepting real love, not a word or a myth, that you will never be hurt again. Yet, when you risk going into the deep unknown, that is where you find the most happiness.

I really enjoyed sharing "Diving Into the Wreck" with you. I enjoyed learning new words in sign language. I hope you felt the same about the new words you discovered. You and I create our own words and myths to explain our love to each other. I know this is a long way to say I love you, but three words are not enough to express the love I feel for you.

Tiffany

Kathleen,

I awoke with the taste of your mouth, your flesh, your touch, in my mouth, my brain, my hands, my eyes, my everything. All day I remembered and smiled quietly to myself.

I spoke softly to others.

Everything reminded me of you.

The blush on a frosty pink rose.

The resonant intensity of blue lobelia standing staunchly in a terracotta pot under the golden chain tree.

The sky, the sun, the cool clear breeze.

The fullness of September.

profusions of clear color: of roses

of lavender and white impatiens
of misty, heatherish caryopterous
of deep blue veronica and salvia.

Everything shining, new and clear, calling to me: "I am the Earth. This is my fullness, my beauty, my everything."

And the Earth's exuberance is mine also.

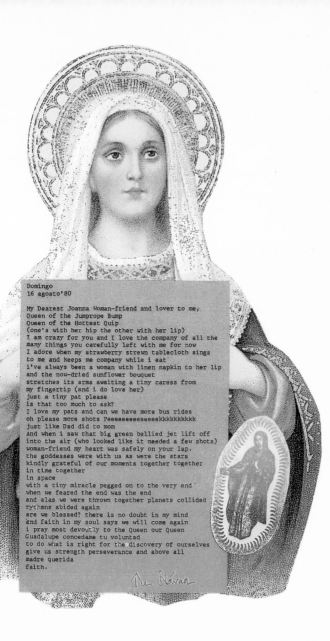

```
Domingo
16 agosto'80

My Dearest Joanna Woman-friend and lover to me;
Queen of the Jumprope Bump
Queen of the Hottest Quip
(one's with her hip the other with her lip)
I am crazy for you and I love the company of all the
many things you carefully left with me for now
I adore when my strawberry strewn tablecloth sings
to me and keeps me company while i eat
i've always been a woman with linen napkin to her lip
and the now-dried sunflower bouquet
stretches its arms awaiting a tiny caress from
my fingertip (and i do love her)
just a tiny pat please
is that too much to ask?
I love my pats and can we have more bus rides
oh please more shots Peeeeeeeeeeeeeeekkkkkkkkkk
just like Dad did to mom
And when i saw that big green bellied jet lift off
into the air (who looked like it needed a few shots)
woman-friend my heart was safely on your lap.
the goddesses were with us as were the stars
kindly grateful of our moments together together
in time together
in space
with a tiny miracle pegged on to the very end
when we feared the end was the end
and alas we were thrown together planets collided
rythmns abided again
are we blessed? there is no doubt in my mind
and faith in my soul says we will come again
i pray most devoutly to the Queen our Queen
Guadalupe concedame tu voluntad
to do what is right for the discovery of ourselves
give us strength perseverance and above all
madre querida
faith.
```

Dear Mabel

Read your letter and was very glad to hear from you and to know that you have been well and happy. This leaves me feeling better then I have felt since you left. Not sure about going away but if I do Michel will be taken care of. No I haven't comb her hair as she won't let me, but she is being

a nice child. She and I are getting along fine. Well everything is o.k. at home only this time I and Michel miss you so much will be glad when the time is up. I am writing this on my lunch hour. It is 11 pm now. I am quitting tomorrow.

Don't see anyone as I haven't been feeling any too well. Hope everyone is well. Regard to Mrs. Nathan and your new friends. If I go to Boston I will leave Sat. nite. Well the half of hour is up now. Nite nite be good and will see you soon.

Little Bear

639 & 169st

Br_____ N.Y

Hello d_____

hope _____ will

be home _____

left 20 _____

been ve_____

MISS

Lilian Foster

#639 EAST 169TH ST.

BRONX 56, NEW YORK.

send you your books as a _____

over

Patricia,

I love you. I said those words to you this morning, but lest you think that I now recite that lover's litany by rote, I want to tell you again. I love you. But it wasn't so long ago that I didn't. Forty-three days ago, over drinks and a virtually ignored quesadilla, I was infatuated with you. I thought you were cute, clever, and eccentrically charming. I wanted to get to know you better.

Six weeks later, much has changed. I still find you attractive and witty. I remain drawn to your idiosyncratic approach to life. And there is still so much that I want to know about you. But now I love you. And when I say those words to you, as I did this morning, it is more than a lifeless recitation, the same tired muscular path that my lips have traveled many times. It is the fresh expression of my captivated heart. You deserve nothing less.

Robin

...oo3-24-87oo...

Rebecca,

This is your (OFFICIAL) invitation
to join me on One Friday April night; to
A) celebrate our Love + affection,
B) Allow you to watch me dance with other women,
c) To rub my body up against yours in a slow dance,
D) To laugh with you and enjoy each others' presence,
E) To tie you up, and make love to you, Quickly!

Now you've been officially invited.
you can,
A) Ignore this pathetic plea,
B) Chose a suitable Night,
c) Dream about tying me up, making me helpless while you eat me,
d) Make a jello mold, or tofu treat,
E) Call me, or run or sleep,
F) Buy me a ring,
G) Do some dishes.
H) Masturbate like there's no tomorrow,
I) Sweat impulsively,
J) Emit a small portion of gas.   You decide.

Love you —
Jew Girl

83

Dearest, Panther would cast many spells if you were here.
He purred and better purred over the words you wrote. . . .
He could see you, dreaming in that sunny spot—didn't
you hear him sniffing the air, and turning in the fading

grasses . . . shoving his nose gently
through the Dryad's leaves. Surely, oh
surely, with such a strong desire in our
hearts to make each other happy, the
Fates will not be unkind. I love you not

only for the flaming moments when I seek to give and take
all that is hidden in the heart of passion, when kisses
resemble the burning caresses clouds bestow on mountains
ere they sleep. The subtlety of spiritual passion flows like
a deep river through our life together . . . I hope you can be
happy with me—I am with you—The world has been
unkind to me in some ways, as you know, and I am
sensitive when misunderstood—our own "kind" being the
only ones who can judge us fairly. For years I lived among
aliens, and that, I suppose has left me different than the
rather shy but buoyant being I used to be . . . My courage
is still there, but my reserve is greater . . . Panther longs
for you, and looks forward to your return . . . You often
slip in at door, rustling gently, and the leaves enfold the

Panther until there is only <u>greenness</u> visible and wavering shadows on the wall!—I enjoy all your descriptions of your doings. Don't write when you are too tired dear . . . It is true I am lonely, but I do not grudge you one minute's absence—there are, I hope, years ahead of us, and happy ones at that. . . . There is a lovely article on "Cat-Worship" in October "Cornhill Magazine." . . .

Pierrot, sitting on my lap, rubbing my face . . . He sends you a loving bite. The imp— eating salmon—looks up to send her love. Now I am going to read. . . . Does Panther's shade kiss you softly in the mornings? The Imp is now sitting on the back of my neck, purring, like a witch's cat, and softly treading her Joy!—So, I take you nearest my furry heart and kiss you. You know the rest—Dryad's magic and Panther's spells commingle! Goodnight!

Darling,

I will continue on the path like a true warrior. I release you into the great sea of love from whence you first came to me. We will meet again. I love you eternally. I am committed to your soul forever.

You will never be farther from me than my heart, where you have a permanent resting place, free from fear, free from judgment.

I love you <u>unconditionally</u>. I am in your life to serve your soul. We have completed our first journey together in this lifetime. We have come together. We have infused each other with love & strength & wisdom.

We have empowered one another, inspired and nurtured. You are very beloved to me, my precious wonder! I trust the future. I am excited to see what will happen next. I love living my vision. I let go of wanting you. I let go of my attachment to you.

I will miss holding you . . . You are the most powerful lover I have ever had in this lifetime & I surrendered to you completely with no fantasies other than of your energies merging and mingling with mine creating a cauldron of synergy out of which peace and justice is fed to the planet.

We have done some very good work together my darling comrade. The entire world has been uplifted by our partnership, by our love.

I have grown immeasurably with you & I see how far I still must go in this lifetime. So, I trust the future.

Love,

Your Catherine

Mi amor:

I haven't stopped loving you but the pain of our relationship has turned me into a despicable, overly sensitive and insecure creature. . . . And two pimples erupted on my left forearm; I know it's because of us. I HATE MYSELF. I told you once that I didn't know if I could forgive you for betraying me. I tried to let it go and believe that you were more confused than dishonest. Still, I DON'T TRUST YOU. That stained white cap you wore when we

first met turned me off, and so did that cheap looking knotted gold earring. Your soft, low, polite voice and the way you fold your hands when you speak made me tag you as insecure, conservative, and unimaginative. I DIDN'T EVEN LIKE YOU AT FIRST. I agreed to have sex with you because I had pre-menstrual horniness and I needed a good fuck to get the blood flowing. I didn't think you'd be any good in bed because you bored me with your talk of "caressing" women. But I figured it was worth the risk because we'd never see each other again and anyway, when you squeezed my thigh for an instant in that bus, I immediately oozed. WE SHOULD HAVE JUST FUCKED AND LEFT IT AT THAT. You told me

that you didn't love her anymore and that the magic had worn off. You portrayed her as an immature, manipulative alcoholic who didn't even please you in bed . . . You wanted out, but you were never brave enough to leave. YOU LIED TO ME. At first I thought that the close relationship you had with your family was due to mutual love and business ties. Now I see that you let them devalue your work, control your money, limit your life and our love, and humiliate you for being a lesbian. I LOST MY RESPECT FOR YOU. I believed in our dreams of sharing a life together. Feeling tiny in my king-size bed, I made a space that waited for you. I wore your ugly knotted gold earring like a trophy. I HATE YOU FOR MAKING ME LOSE FAITH IN LOVE.

One day not too long ago I fell in love with a woman. I didn't try to or anything — it just happened. So now I am a Lesbian. Some would choose to view me differently now because I have a new label. Seems to me that the only thing different about me is that I'm in love, & before I wasn't.

So here I am, hanging out in a brand new scene — seeing, feeling, knowing new things. First time I went to an all-woman dance the most impressive thing I felt was the gentle loving energy flowing thruout. Women were dancing, laughing, liking, loving together. It's beautiful, this women-loving-women.

In spite of all the positive feelings growing within me, there is outrage sprouting. Seems that because I'm in love, there's pressure from the mainstream to become invisible. Well, I'm not invisible — so I think I'll just keep being me. I feel like the best thing for me to do is be in love until I'm not.

Sue

Droopy and Sad

made
Perky
and Glad

Dear Chelle

I sat behind you tonight, riding back to your home, reflecting on a day of observing you in all the roles you fill — mother, grandmother, wife . . . watching for myself the joy this grandbaby . . . brings to your life . . . watching how you struggle with being "mom" to 3 grown women . . . what a delicate balance that must always be for you . . . Sitting back here in this seat watching you: foot against the dash, arm laid casually over bent knee, fingers occasionally moving through your soft graying hair; wanting to touch you, to put my hands through your hair, to put my arms around your shoulders, to feel connected to you in the silence.

Yesterday I did that for the moment we stood watching the sun set from a bluff at your sacred childhood place; for a moment touching you and that place — a connection, a picture I want to store deep for memories sake.

Feeling sad as I reflect on what I saw today . . . the reality of knowing I may have a unique and special place in your life but it won't ever be to the fullness my deepest self desires it. Your joy is here with your family; a joy I couldn't give you no matter how hard I tried. . . . perhaps being in this place of desiring what I can't have from you will pass, or at least I will pass through to another place I can't see right now . . . but for this moment, I just need to allow the sadness in; the personal emptiness I can't seem to find a way to fill. Maybe if I let the tears come, they will clear my vision and show me where to go from here.

Loving,

Cathy

My Sweet Lover—

It's Saturday & it's cold & windy outside. Once again the temperature has dropped and it feels bitter. Makes me want to stay in. But I did change clothes today. I looked through the blue clothes "vats" and found new/old clothes. I'm all in black, black rayon pants, black turtleneck, black shoes. . . . It looks cool but I have to wear coats, scarves, gloves to go outside so I might as well be in p.j.'s.

I LOVE YOU . . .

So, Janet called, she said she was really hung over so it's taking awhile for her to pull it together. She'll probably come over tonight . . .

YOU'RE MY WIFE . . .

I've been experimenting w/eye make-up. Specifically, darkening my eyebrows. Except I don't have any eyebrow-pencil so I use gold/brown eyeshadow (yours). It works. Then I use the same shadow on my eyes—subtle, but makes my eyes look more . . . more.

AND I POSSESS YOU . . .

And, I did my nails—I used clear polish and my nails are growing and they look better. . . . Not that I would allow them to <u>interfere</u> w/soft tissues on the likes of you, my sweet baby.

94

*SO DO AS I SAY & I'LL SHOW YOU PLEASURE . . .
AND PAIN . . .*

*Did you know that "Thirty-something" is also on on
Saturdays? . . . I've been faithfully taping the 11 p.m.
shows. Only for you, my love.*

*TAKE DOWN YOUR PANTIES . . . ALL THE WAY DOWN — I
WANT YOU TO EXPOSE YOURSELF TO ME — SHOW ME YOUR
VERY <u>PRIVATE</u> PARTS.*

There's been a bunch of fucked up painters workin' in the building . . Real stupid looking. I try to be civil, but I hate them.

LET ME KISS YOUR SWEET LIPS, MY BABY. LET ME PUT MY TONGUE INSIDE YOUR MOUTH. LET ME TASTE YOU, MOVE MY MOUTH INSIDE OF YOURS.

I'm making chili. It smells good. I just went down to get the mail. Citibank says we can get a free gift now. People mag came . . . The phone bill. We're doing better. $144.00. But I'm afraid this month might shoot us back up there. I've been trying to talk less to you, but I can't help it. . . .

BE READY FOR ME, BABY. THERE WILL BE NO TIME TO RELAX WHEN YOU ARRIVE HOME. UNLESS YOU CONSIDER IT RELAXING TO BE SPREAD OPEN, HANDS TIED, ASS EXPOSED TO ME.

I cut my bangs. I look a little like a Beatle b/c I have been letting it dry straight but slightly "mussed". I love you, my darlin'—Hurry home.

R.

Donna,

*I held your
hand all morning
and felt your
dreams in
your fingertips
in your
warm thighs.*

*You were truly
gorgeous last
nite, honey.
Just dazzling.*

Sleep sweet.

I kiss you.

Cayenne—I'm really glad you responded to my e-mail. God, this is a hard one (coming to terms with my femme-self). In some ways although I wear my "femmeness" on my sleeve (so to speak)—I still grapple with it on an intellectual and emotional level. As a child I always liked typical girl femmey things—dolls, dresses—and didn't like butchy things—sports, rough housing etc. . . . In fact, girls that I grew up with that I now recognize as butch, I was afraid of and I steered clear. (Could it be that I "knew" of my forbidden desires even then?)

I came out as a lesbian in '84—wow already 10 years. . . . At first it was more of a curiosity than a burning desire. . . . From the start I was always attracted to butch dykes. I would notice a beautiful woman—and still do—but in a completely different way than a handsome woman. When I look at femme dykes my thought process is something like "She's beautiful, I wonder what that hair cut would look like on me . . ." When I see a butch dyke I don't think, my body responds. . . .

I tried to deny my attraction to butch dykes and even went through years of trying to be butch myself. I tried this because it was not p.c. or acceptable, and women that

I met would always ask me if I was bi or straight . . . It really pissed me off. I felt like I was always having to prove that I was a dyke . . . At any rate, about 3–4 years ago I started to reassess things. I began to realize that I could no more change myself  *to make myself butch or andro than I could change my attraction to butchy dykes. Not only that—but I didn't want to change either one of these. I realized that this dynamic . . . is as much a part of me as my soul itself. It is a part of me at the innermost level and I finally began . . . to nurture and explore it. I've decided that I don't want to settle for anything other than what my soul desires, which is a butch complement to my femme-self. An equal (but different) partner. So I'm waiting until I meet her . . .*

How about your "coming out" as a butch—what has that been like for you? . . . I was pleased to get your e-mail yesterday and look forward to hearing from you soon. (I'll be waiting in my impatient femme-way.) How did you choose the name Cayenne & what is your real name?

Gigi

Beth,

To me, this is not only important, but the fact that it exists is unequivocally <u>neat</u>! So, here goes:

I have a real appreciation for your values and the total part that they play in shaping all of your exchanges and interactions with that which, individually and collectively, comprises life! . . . Being able to know you is in itself a privilege. But being close to you is marvelous indeed.

You must know I love you.

When I see you
my gay heart pounds
with tingles of delight.
Tingles, Tingles, Tingles, Tingles.
Tingles of delight.
And the older I get,
the harder it is to believe.
This can't happen every day!

Gay gay gay gay gay gay

Gay gay gay gay gay

Gay gay!

Debbie

Beloved . . . No letter from you today as yet — this is because there has been a Sunday — I am growing to dread the weekends . . . It seems so strange and so terribly wrong not to be able to talk to you, not to be able to discuss things together . . . Last night I had one of my

fits of the glooms. When the weight of life lay heavy upon me, when everything seemed dust and ashes in my mouth, when I felt that I had not made good at all, that I never would make good being what I am — that the scales were too heavily weighted against me — I get like this sometimes and have done for years — it is the melancholy of the inverted. I tell you this because it is God's truth that you can lift me right out of such moods, that when I am lying in your arms and you in mine such moods cannot touch me, that you, Soulina, can make me forget the great weariness of spirit, mind & body that I feel sometimes — I feel battle-weary, and you are my rest, my joy, and my ultimate justification. When I am with you I am younger than you are, I am young and carefree and irresponsible in nearly all things save your happiness; I am back where I was many years ago with only one

difference—*I know that I am kinder & more considerate & understanding. Oh, well, it may be that I should be glad that life has knocked me about a bit if because of this it has made John a more worthy & steadfast love for Soulina. Dearest I must stop. . . . God bless you my rest, my joy and my hope. . . .*

Your John

Dearest Judy,

It's late in the night. I'm tired, yet I can't go to sleep. Have you ever lain in your bed, your head lost in the pillow . . . your teeth clenched tight so that they'll keep you from screaming out loud—all because you miss somebody so very much? It's a miserable feeling. My eyes cry desperately for sleep, they are ready to close and die away. But my mind can't. Thoughts . . . violate its peace, like a swirling tornado. And one persistent thought keeps imposing itself on the others: I want to see her. Please, I've got to see her.

Something stirs inside my chest. Like a hand gripping my heart, suffocating me. I want to breathe hard and fast, I want to cry. Where are the tears? Even <u>they</u> don't come. Nothing comes. God! Is it possible to miss someone so much? . . . I know that first thing tomorrow morning I'll call you, because I must talk to you.

I remember what you said the other night—that you're scared . . . So am I . . . But I'm also desperately in love. In love with everything in you and about you. In love with your thoughts, in love with your face, in love with your feelings and emotions. Is it wrong to feel this way? . . . Do you feel the same way? . . . All I know is that right now the way I feel is the way of my life. And I've always believed that there's nothing I care more about than the way of my life.

There must be something wrong with the world, I think. Why should we be afraid of what we feel, of what we think? Why should they be right and we wrong? . . . It's not just a matter of a woman falling in love with another woman, it's a whole way of approaching life, a whole series of beliefs and ideals, and feelings that is at stake. And I'm too selfish, too self-confident, to accept theirs instead of mine. In a way, I'm scared only because you are. I don't want to cause you any trouble . . . But for myself I don't care. I'm in love. What does it matter whether it's a man or a woman? Love is wonderful, marvelous, beautiful in all its forms and aspects. Love is love.

I love you, Judy. I say it and I don't care, I'm not ashamed. I want to say it again and again. I love you Judy. Judy, I love you.

Charoula

D.

I am wearing red. My mouth dives into your hidden redness. I am red, full of red blood, dripping clear on white sometimes. My red sweater is stretched by you — you fill my enlarging self. I kiss your red mouth; as I leave your lips, the threads of saliva still bind us for a moment longer, and I see our connection. I hate it when the threads go back into each one's mouth; my threads want to touch again. I want to feel that colorless air that flows into us, breathing life and love, pregnant inside — growing love inside — growing myself inside — nurturing you inside me — loving you inside me — feeling you next to me.

R.

10/14/86

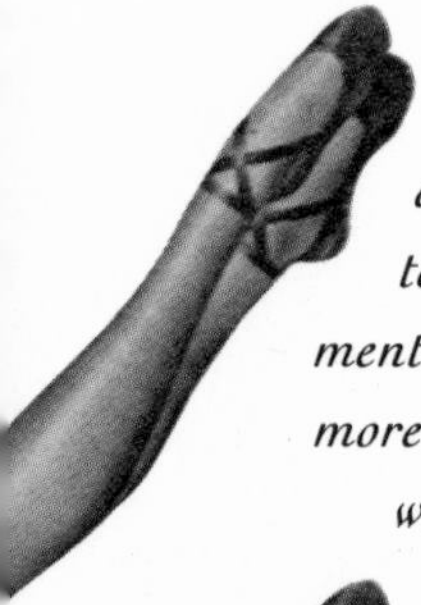
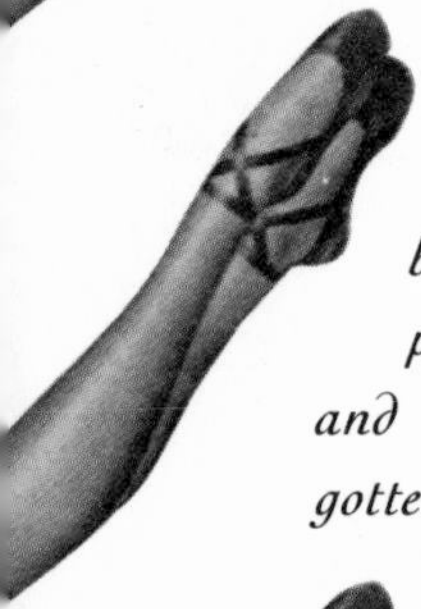

Dearness,

Hey, I know we could be all in each other's boundaries and set some, like, bad precedents—get some bad habits going now. But I don't think we're going to do it. I get this sense that we're both a little too aware these days of the whole process, a sufficient amount of healthy to not get too wrapped up. It's tempting, but it's not. . . . I am liking you sexually, mentally, emotionally. But I know there's a whole lot more to know before I want to get a lot of my habits wrapped up with a lot of yours. . . . Still, I am thrilled about the opportunity of getting to know you more. I know a lot of that, despite the illusion, no matter how expressive we are to each other, cannot be rushed. It takes time to know. There's time and patience here. I trust my ability to take care of me and not rush into something before I've consciously gotten the information so I can purposefully decide. I think you are at that age and stage of wisdom to also want something you can sink your teeth into, something substantive, building, gratifying in the near future and out there a little, something that adds to where you've been before, something that

won't be a discussion
that comes to an end
too soon. I believe you
are looking for that and
that you will take the time to
figure out whether I am,
in fact, that. No matter
how hot we feel about each
other right now. . . . neither of us
knows how we need to play out
in the other's life. I have a
real trust about me, about
time, and about you, which I
think can guide the coming months
of discovery and minimize an
unhealthy idealization/codependency.
My red flags are still there for
checking out. So are yours.

I feel on top of it. Trusting the
process, yes. Thinking about that
flannel pajama top . . .

Joanne

ON A PEDESTAL

My Imperial Love,

What if I had not touched the napkin to my lips and seen your note? Would there still be forty-four years between us? Now there is floral tissue. Dear hortiphile, you know how permeable I am to wet language. So age is just a matter of experience, and some of us are more experienced than others? Well, how delightfully true, and I LOVE being your favorite "thermosexual."

I think I made love with you at first sight. Remember when you picked me up at the depot? It was 1970. You were only seventy then. You wore your long hair coiled in a crown round your head. At every curve of the road, you sounded your horn.

For me, the fusion was so swift, my body always knew it could only catch up more slowly—like fifteen years give or take a few moons. This unlimited longing was the sweetest marrow in my bones. Time is my inhalant, carrying your colors in its fragrance.

If I indeed "kindle your french," please know your tongue glistens miracles in me. Thank you for widening heaven.

Is the Goddess House ever so happy as when Her girls come back flushed with love? Void filled to the brim?

Yr,

Celeste

Sheri dear, (redundant?)

I thought of you 1 million x last night—at Lucie Blue Tremblay (I was sleeping); in the Belly Bowl having a midnite snack w/Kay and checking out babes (Butch Watch); trying to zip myself in "necked"; and, of course, sleeping downhill. . . . I have met a few dykes sitting in the dining tent shooting the shit and eating the shit (actually, ask someone w/a sense of taste about the food—it's bland but OK if you ask me). . . . I look forward to checking out the "main" camp (there are only 4,000 dykes here now, but that will probably double by Sat.). It's chilly enough for a coat and the sun is not really out yet. Nudity is truly a goal for me and I am praying to Aphrodite for sunshine. My outfits definitely fall short of the fabulous lesbo look all around me. But fashion worries will be over when I can take off my clothes. So many sisters are even working their morning outfits. Once again I am ashamed of my circa '85 black thing.

I try to see you here in long johns, overalls, rubbers, flannel, womon-crafted jewelry, a vinyl poncho (invaluable), and a smile. I think you'd love "the Land." It truly is the greatest collection of lesbian beauty and

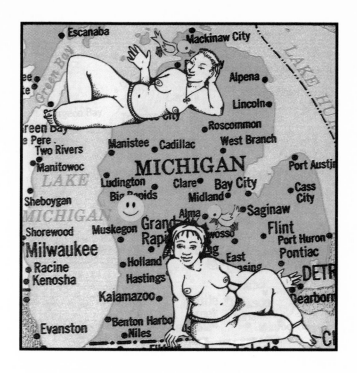

diversity I have ever encountered. It's overwhelming at first—you have to get over feeling hopelessly goofy, uncool, badly or wrongly dressed, and disconnected from the scene. When you relax you see, of course, fabulous babes, but you also see women you'd probably be friends w/back home. And there's lots of bitchy intrigue! ...

Now it's Nighttime. The evening show has the festival in a frenzy. Tribe 8 ("let's fuck some shit up!") has some womyn in a dither because of "violence." The trouble is that they aren't violent. Okay, they hacked a strap-on dildo off Lynn, the lead singer, w/a big weapon during a song about gang castration. They are loud and thrashing (the 1st Michigan mosh pit was designated tonite), but they are not even that far out. Maybe Gibby-Haynes-looking dykes freak out the mainstream, but on the Land? It's stupid. . . .

I'm regretting that the endlessly filling cup of coffee (filling up and spilling over) is making me have to use the Port-o-Jane so fucking often. Trust me — it stinks. Everybody squats on the land after dark, though — they just don't talk about it.

When do we get to fuck? Being around all this unbridled beauty and lust has me wondering. Amidst all this clamoring lezzieness, your beauty and desirability remain unsurpassed. Sheri, turn me out —

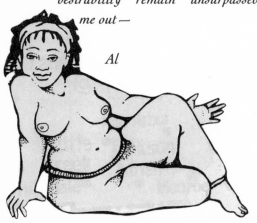

Al

What shall I do when the postman fails to bring me a letter everyday, dearest? It did not come by this morning's mail and although I had said to myself that of course I should not have one today, nevertheless work dragged a little because it failed to come. This afternoon mine was ready for him to take and as a reward, he gave me yours. It takes me one-half second to tear open the envelope and then, darling, I literally <u>devour</u> the contents. . . . my darling, is it not strange that each should find inspiration in that other—I cannot understand how I can be an inspiration to you, but I can see full well why <u>you</u> inspire my every day as you do, so that all my life is different for me. Darling, you are more lovely in nature and in every respect than I—do not ever say that you are not "worthy." It is I who am not worthy of the woman who constantly brings to my mind those words of Jean Inglebrook's, "A sweeter woman ne'er drew breath." No, a sweeter woman never did, nor a truer, braver, sincerer, nobler woman! You are all that to me, dear heart, and far, far more. You and my mother are enshrined in my heart as the dearest women God ever made. . . .

My heart is simply overflowing with love for you dearest—if you should be taken out of my life, it would kill me; perhaps not physically—people do live, even if the heart dies. You would not give me your love to take it away again—I know _that_, as I know you, but it frightens me to realize how I depend upon this love of yours, and wonder _how_ it is given to me in such richness. I am selfish, my darling, I cannot understand how a mother can endure having her child give her heart to another. You know that there is a side of my love which is very like its mother's for her child, while there is another quality that makes me feel that _I_ am the child looking to you for the protecting, comforting love which you never fail to give. I long to say to you "Pet me, Jeannette" and put my head on your shoulder to be loved and petted as only you can do it. . . . Do you realize what it means to have _you_, this heart of my life, to talk with you as I would with my own soul, to have nothing hid, to feel that we are one? . . . Goodnight, my darling, it is almost ten and I must leave to rest until tomorrow. It is a constant to have this little talk. What will it be to have it with my arms around you, my own little girl? . . .

Your own Mary

My heart is simply over-
flowing with love for
dearest - If you
taken out of
it would kill
physical-
even if

Dear J,

Are you OK? I keep wondering, how could they do this?
To threaten us. I hope it doesn't go any further. I'm so
sorry about this. I just don't understand why — we
aren't hurting anyone.

I just want to see you. I have to see you. Are
you scared, baby? Me too. When we're together I
feel safe. I want to make you feel safe.

Can you come tonight? Even if only for a short
time. Even if you can't come alone.

Please try, please.

Love,

S.

Hi, it's me again. I came across this old letter today. In it I sounded so desperate. I needed to be with you so badly.

Remember when we used only initials in letters? We were so afraid someone would discover us. That all seems so long ago. At times though I still feel that same terror. The terror of misguided hatred.

Today, we are completely different people from those who found each other in high school.

How did we make it through? We've faced obstacles from the very beginning . . . Why did we not just give up?

Maybe I had no other real option . . . From deep down in my soul, I love you. With every part of me, I love you.

I sometimes feel that you are as essential to my survival as air and water. It's as if my real life began ten years ago. I awoke to the bright sunshine after a dark frightening dream.

You are my happiness, my music, my laughter. Thank you for this life.

Happy tenth, angel.

Love,

S.

April 14, 1991

Darling:

2:00 P.M. I miss you. I feel voiceless and very quiet and low. I am in this strange city and I feel paralyzed and marooned. Usually I can just get up and go walking, running, wandering, exploring. . . . I feel as if I've been plucked down in an alien, hostile world. I certainly do not feel social . . . Something is stirring up and around in me. As if I have something to do but can't remember what it is.

10:30 P.M. I have trouble sleeping without you. I try to settle into a dream of you but I am impatient and feel lost. It is quiet and every hour a long empty coal train runs through the city. I went for a run before, just as it was getting dark and as I ran along the river, the train seemed to chase me . . . I want our lives to be simple and harmonious; I imagine our house near the ocean and how it will be to float up out of sleep and feel your warmth, the scent of you in my mind, on my fingers.

I love you, Rue. My wild and wonderfully eclectic lover. My wife. Everything is possible, darling. All of what we're working on will fall into place, will evolve and mature . . . I have never had such a wonderful year: this first year of our marriage and our commitment and our sharing. I

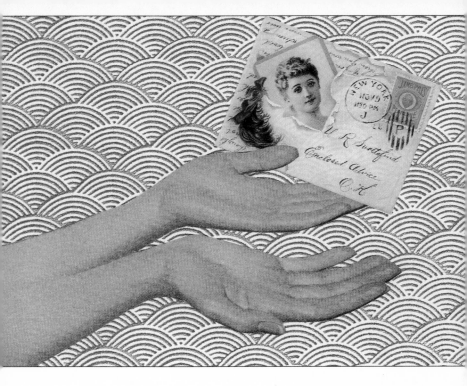

want to thank you for that, Rue. . . . You and Elizabeth,
our beautiful daughter, and me. My family. I am glad to
be coming home.

All my love,

Merry

Ahh, my sweetest Gena—
  how I miss you . . .
Did I ever tell you that I always saw you as a cross
between James Dean and a cold slab of salmon?
  (I have such reverence for the past)
Why am I built for love,
  & then fated to live alone
with a 6 yr. old vibrator
  & nothing but memories?
Happiness these days seems to be the absence of pain.

And I haven't written because I've been INSANE, silly . . .
It's very difficult to gossip . . . when I'm tied in this damn
straight jacket and wish I were dead . . .

  Oh, sorry about that pooky.
The hopelessness just keeps slipping out . . .

TAH!

(And to think I could've been the next Kaye Ballard . . .)

WESSELY

My love my love, I love my love,
My love I love, I love my love,
Bless her, her little fingers and her
big finger and her whole hand and all
of her bless her, I love my love bless
her and the two little apples inside her
bless her, and the cow that comes out
with her, bless her, I love
 my love, my
love I love, bless her.

Dear Roolie,

Isn't it overwhelming to think that two weeks from this very night I will be with you, talking or laughing, or making love. This time I am going to hold you so tightly you'll never get away.

I just finished reading an article on Cyprus. It sounds like a lovely, inexpensive, exciting place. Maybe we could go there? And make sacrifices to the Cypriot queen, Aphrodite. Women pilgrims used to prostitute themselves to the first person willing and give the money to the goddess' treasury. It sounds like someone had a good idea. Now I suppose it is the Virgin Mary. How strangely the goddess of love has been transformed into the lady of sorrows. It's fascinating. The world has aged in the wrong, the joyless way. How I miss you.

Darling, will I need a coat? Perhaps I will bring a sweater for the islands, a bikini for Aphrodite and a cape for Mater Dolorosa.

Gail

You can take my tie
You can take my coller
But I'll jazze you
'Till you holler.

My dearest Wife Gloria:—
I am writing to you because I have not written to you for
so long and sweet heart you will have to forgive me but I
love you just the same; that handchief that you sent is to
pretty to use and I am going to take it out with me when
I go. Honey If you love me you will brake out your dam
door and come an sleep with me and angle face if I could
sleep with you I would not only hough and kiss you. But
I will not take the time to write it for I guess you can
read between lines. When I kiss you I thought I was in
heaven and I was kissing one of the angles, up there if I
were in cuba and you in spain the love I get for you will
make a bool dog break his chain, and I don't care what
you use to be but I know what you are to day if you
love me or I love you what has the world to say. You ask
me no questions so why should I. I don't care whet you
use to be but I know what you are to day. I love you and
you only.

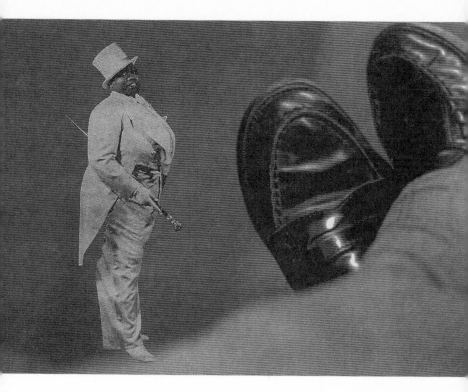

x o x o x o x o x o x o
from your love husben
Ocean love to my wife Gloria love

AN EXUBERANCE, NOT A DUMP

For Zan
I can't give you anything but sex baby
Creamy waves are washing all the decks baby
Come a while — come with style — you'll come to find
happy gales, typhoon tails, hurricanes of climax baby

Sure I'd love to see you making port baby
With some handsome sailor just your sort baby
Till that lucky day here's my report baby
I can't give you anything but sex

I can't give you anything but sex baby
Can't offer you a penthouse or duplex baby
Just a cave in the wave where we can spoon
honey cake that we'll bake — and put lots of cream on
*   baby*

Sure I want to see you shacked up nice baby
with some groovy chick that's worth your price baby
Till that lucky day here's my advice baby
I can't give you anything but sex

Please don't give me anything but cream baby
Most every other thing is only Preem baby
Give me you and your goo—you're such a fish
You're so wet that I'll bet you could fill the whole
    Pacific

Launch those little boats and make 'em rock baby
Don't bother counting stitches in my sock baby
You'll come so big that I won't have to knock baby
Please don't give me anything but cream

May

I am getting sleepy, for I must confess that it is past bed-time. I went to church this morning, but this afternoon I have been far afield, way over the hill and beyond, to an unusual distance. Alas, when I went to see my beloved big pitch-pine tree that I loved best of all the wild tress that lived in Berwick, I found only the broad stump of it beside the spring, and the top boughs of it scattered far and wide. It was a real affliction, and I thought you would be sorry, too, for such a mournful friend as sat down and counted the rings to see how many years old her tree was, and saw the broad rings when good wet summers had helped it grow and narrow ones when there had been a drought, and read as much of its long biography as she could. But the day was very lovely . . . I found such a good little yellow apple on one of the pasture trees, and I laughed to think how you would be looking at the next bite. It was <u>very</u> small but I nibbled it like a squirrel. . . . I was in some underbrush, going along the slope, and saw a crow come toward me flying low, and when I stood still he did not see me and came so close that I could hear his wings creak their feathers . . . I wished for you so much, it was a day you would have loved.

hello baby,

I have to go into the city—Please forgive my brevity. I was again reduced to goose bumps & giggles upon getting your letter & photo! I received a letter from my friend Greta today also & I teased myself by reading the whole thing (5 pgs) while holding your unopened one. As I got to the last page of Greta's I started getting hotter & hotter & more & more excited & found myself in quite a frenzy clawing open your blue envelope, breathless.

Today's Patti Smith's 30th birthday. How I wish you were here with me. (Talk about understatement.) Patti has had ads for her concert on the radio—they're great! She's talking & saying stuff like "Help us fight the good fight," and "Come NY's eve and help us ring in a pair of sevens!" Television and John Cale are also great—I can't think of a better show really. I've been listening to a lot of radio ... & unfortunately am hearing millions of albums that we can't live without. Were you ever a T. Rex fan? They were my life for a few months in high school. . . .

I'll give Patti a smooch for you tonight if the opportunity arises . . . Oh Helen—can't you hear me knockin'? I love you forever!—Carole

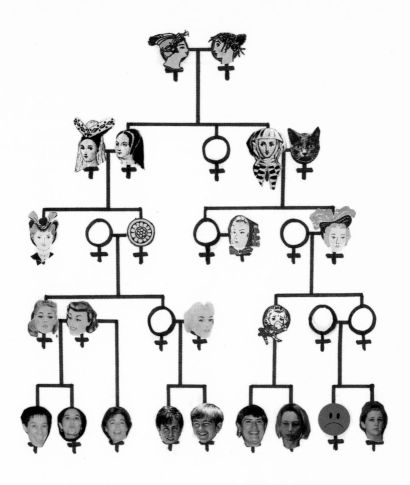

P.S. John found you <u>very</u> cute & intelligent. And the 2 of us, blatantly and passionately attracted to one another. A keen appraisal, no?

Darling Wendy or Wendy Darling —
I'm in a limo driving to sound check thinking of you, of
Sunny, of the bridge we just went over. We've been gone a
day, but as in heaven — a day is as a thousand. Perhaps
not to you, but I've already done two planes; two shows;
2 hotels; thousands of people; 3 showers; 1 in-store;
8 different limos; 3 different promoters; a hundred
autographs; 2 strippers; 60 photographs; 4 interviews;
3 mini-stores for food; 2 meals; 4 bunches of flowers;
7 roses; lots of phone #'s (I told everyone about you);
4 shots of Jagermeister; 1 buttery nipple; 5 different
tapes all the way through; 2 sound checks; 7 bottles of
water; 1 blown speaker; 1 mic stand explosion;

and a million thoughts of You. I'm tired. It's raining —
warm & wet — sound familiar? I'd kiss this, but it won't
do a damn bit of good — I never wear lipstick do I? Is this
absurd? Are we — am I? I'm in Office Depot to touch you
with my writing.

Kisses,

Christina

Textile Cone *Conus textile*

Dear Laura,

Hello, my dear. Thanks for
the ___ card by your ___
___ happy for you
___ soul to be
___ "refreshing" wat___
___ who under
___

___ dream —
___ flying over th___
___

STATES OF
___NESIA 50¢

FEDERATED STATES OF
MICRONESIA

___ you
___ne, seein
___ stat___

___ had a rea___
___ being up in hig___
___ student, lookin
___ wing

I love you more deeply than
there are words.

Federated States of
Micronesia 1¢
Rooses Reef

Federated States of
Micronesia 1¢

REPUBLIK INDONESIA
TOURIST PASS
KEPPRES 15/83
VALID FOR TWO MONTHS FROM
BERLAKU UNTUK 2 BULAN DARI

1 9 JUN 1993

EMPLOYMENT PROHIBITED
DILARANG BEKERJA
NGURAH RAI
IMMIGRATION OFFICER

Visas   Departures/Sorties
Entries/Entrées

Hey,

Well it's been a little time since this pen hit the paper. Maybe it's been a denial, if I don't write I won't think of her. Sure. Nice try. So let's see, since my last letter, I've become a woman with a pierced tongue. . . . it's sore now like a bruised muscle. It's kinda a rush. . . . I'll send you a picture of my tongue soon. . . .

. . . What do you think will become of us? You and me. Sometimes I don't even care about all of that. I just want you at that moment. I want to run my tongue all over your body. Stopping along the way, maybe at your nipples. Slow licks, little sucks, littler bites. One big mouthful every now and then. Then my hand slides down your belly stopping at the rim of your undies. Over or under, it's always a tough decision. I skip to your inner thigh, it's so soft. I feel a little moisture on my hand as it runs through your legs. This makes my clit hard. That first feel of your hairy pussy, not the lips just the hair. There's nothing like it. Then the first move for the wetness. Slowly, not too fast, makes you really want it. That one finger pushes its way deep in the spirit. The darkness, the sweet smell overcomes us both. We kiss. Can you feel the little metal ball on my tongue. Imagine

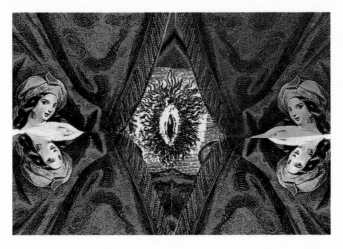

it on your pussy. The smoothness of it. Word is, it feels great. Right now we can only imagine. Where was I? Somewhere in your pussy. How many fingers? Who cares? It feels wonderful. You're bottomless. You could suck me in all the way. At this point some of our most pleasureful sexual encounters flood my memory. Like the one in Yvona's room. . . . You got right up on my face. No covers. WHOA DOG. . . . Now I got to cut this out. I must get these devil thoughts from my head. Now you have a swell day, Trudy. I miss you like crazy. You get on back here, girl. I want my secret lover closer to me. Stay healthy, baby.

Dez

My darling—

You are still near me—where I can fold you in my arms at any moment and press your sweet clinging lips—but the desolation of bereavement is stealing over me—and I must write for if I speak we can neither one be brave . . . I have tried to tell you what you are to me but no words can say it—If you love me ask your own heart what mine says—then add to it that bliss of freedom I have felt with you—that perfect understanding—no reserve, no concealment, no simulation—but—whether we played on the hilltops or by the singing brook—or whether in our beloved cabin—we were locked in the strongest—holiest embrace. All was most perfect and spontaneous bliss—

Shall I ever again see rocks and trees without thinking of you—hearing your thrilling voice as you told me of yourself or asked the deepest questions of life—Shall I ever stand in the moonlight without seeing and feeling beside me the white sweet flower of my perfect bride—my pure bride.

If I could only go away alone and think of it all. I should be content—should have enough to live on for my life . . . oh my darling—you have made life a glory to me—have made me live—and I will think of nothing

else . . . I hold you close — I kiss your breath away — I take you — soon.

Your lover,

Margaret

My Lovely Lady,
Was so good to talk to you yesterday. . . . I just don't
know about myself these days . . . I was discovering the
fun of being "on the make" again . . . Enjoyed flirting
and some short and sweet affairs with no guilt/no
commitment. I was truly living from one party to the
next, one dance to one beer to one lover to another
and it was absolutely good for me. . . .

And suddenly this soft-faced woman pulls me
down from a whirl and hands me her already-
prepared address. . . . Casually, (with subtle
aggression) her words pull me into her life. . . .
"polygamous marriage" . . . "thirty years old" . . . "never
been to gay bars" . . . "lonely" . . . Not just the words, the
tone of voice—soothing, balanced. . . . But take care,
Barb, she goes deep . . . You talk to her in letters and she
responds with tantalizing nuances of rich feelings and
experiences and knowledge . . . just waiting for you . . . to
match with your own. DANGER ZONE!!!

. . . Now I pace a new shoreline, as my sea lady
beckons. I've felt the froth and the waves at my thighs . . .
No morbid undertow lurks. No barracuda teeth or airless
lungs . . . Then why not take the plunge, Barb? Why do

HOTEL MENSES

3030 East 30th Street
New York, New York 30303
Phone (212) 303 3030
Cable address: HotflowNYC

Ms. Maxine Pad, Director

Your urbane menstrual hut in the Big Apple, always warm and welcoming.
Please reserve well in advance of onset of PMS. Inquire about weekend group rates.

you stand hands in pockets, back to the wind . . . ? The gulls scream, "Fall in deep, fall in long . . ."

    But goddamn it to hell, Jan, I can't do it . . . I don't trust the intensity. . . . your incredible perception and skills in knowing people could lay me wide open. As much as I might want that to happen someday, it is too frightening to think about right now . . . I don't know if this fucking letter makes sense to you, especially since it's written to me. But I need you to know how I'm thinking. . . . If this sounds terribly depressing to you, you must realize it's almost time for my period. Doesn't make it all less real or less felt . . . just less threatening.

I need you, woman.

B

Wait until the 23rd
Yes I'll be on my way
We have a date
It's really great
Knowing I'll get laid
You make me come
I'll make you hum
And shake and sweat
And shimmy
And sing
And secrete sweet
    sauce
From your sizzling
    stuff
So sweet sugar
8 days

Chazak— Dearest D.,

When I came from school today and saw there was no mail I felt very sad. My only hope was the afternoon mail. When it came, I ran down the stairs, looked in the box. Only a letter from my brother, my heart almost stopped. But then I looked once more and there it was. I grabbed it, kissed it, flung myself on the couch and began reading it. Oh, it is the most wonderful feeling . . .

If you come out Rosh Hashanah, we shall try to go to the park or somewhere alone. Nature will be our only companion. Then how about having a service all our own, just for ourselves. My conception of our type of service would be plans for the coming year instead of prayers to repent about last year. We can do many things in our service — what do you think? . . .

I have a <u>sicha G'dud</u> in just a few minutes and I must hurry. Please write me as often as possible and I shall do the same. I find when I have a letter from you and you to look forward to it makes the day much brighter . . .

Chazak V'Amatz,

Y

Celeste,

. . . Through my baptismal Catholicism this year I am to sacrifice, in place of sweets or cigarettes, my lack of intimacy towards you. On this day, the beginning of Lent, out of meekness I am sworn to endure intimacy with you. From this day, and for the next forty days, I hold this promise true.

As I kneel, how divine my suffering for this our first kiss on Ash Wednesday.

I will, to pay penance for my faith, have to be one with you until . . . Christ rises from his tomb. Six weeks of sharing mandated by superior beings—I am only a follower. HALLELUJAH! HALLELUJAH! There is a God. I care not if Easter comes.

Dana

Silken One—

. . . Oh BJ—Very, very long sigh! At my desk—you've been gone only a short time . . . Thinking of you in your coat—car should be warm now—driving thru the night. So many feelings mixed around, what to do? Stirrings & feelings & fears and I hope mixed in with all of that a <u>knowing</u> of this spot of comfort for you. My arms are open to hold you near whenever, <u>whenever</u> you feel you wish to be in them—

Am still in some kind of state of shock—images flooding my synapses—still feeling sensations—not knowing what I'm feeling—seeing us. Feeling the warmth of your cheeks against my breasts, holding you on the love seat—nestled against you—feeling the different heat from the passage of your breath as you rest against me & so naturally having your hand move to clear a passage for us thru buttons and silken shirts and me so hesitant & yet not hesitant at all really to clear passage also from gentle wool to silken body. Image after image after image. Can't process these feelings—can only feel them right now & continue to think of you driving in darkness . . .

*Never, I
guess, does this
event ever come to pass
in quite the fantasy way.
Reality is clearly the <u>best</u> of
all. I can't write now—will go
instead to curl in my blanket on the
love seat where we spent such precious time today . . . to
snuggle down into our blended fragrances. . . . likely you
are nearly to South River now. . . . Perhaps it is to my
altar I'll actually go, at least until my watch tells me
you are home, to spend these last moments of your return
trip with you in that way . . .*

Most beautiful woman—I love you—

Jan Elizabeth

Dear Leila—I'm returning the jewelry. I thank you for trusting me to have it—to share it—to wear it. But we talk about completion—for me to return it symbolizes a completion—a completion of our relationship at least as I have known it to be and have wanted it to be. The return is not accompanied by any anger or bitterness. There is some regret that we haven't been able to participate more fully together in this act of separating—But I think I'm prepared to accept your emotional withdrawal—I haven't been so equipped previously. I'm astounded though at how plugged in I am to our relationship—my fantasies, my dreams, my expectations. You are right— an honest, objective analysis of what we've been together and what we are today indicates that a future together is futile—who knows what will happen. I'm not prepared to even guess, I don't want to dream, I don't want to work very hard now at creating or shaping a future together. Undoubtedly something will develop—I think our love for one another runs too deep to just wander out of each others lives—For now I just need some space to be, to heal—I love you deeply,

L.

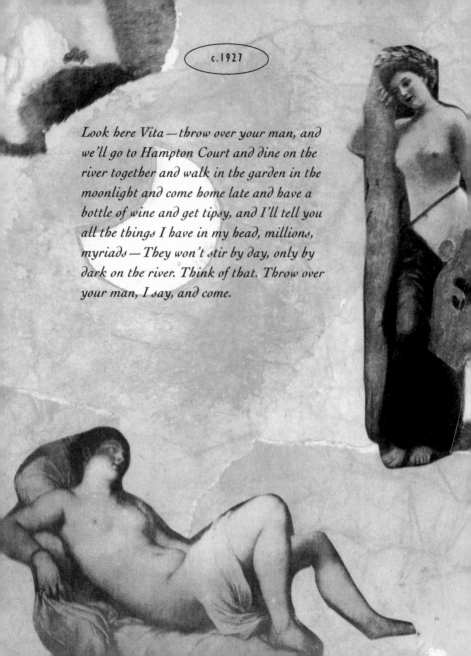

c.1927

Look here Vita—throw over your man, and we'll go to Hampton Court and dine on the river together and walk in the garden in the moonlight and come home late and have a bottle of wine and get tipsy, and I'll tell you all the things I have in my head, millions, myriads—They won't stir by day, only by dark on the river. Think of that. Throw over your man, I say, and come.

ABOUT THE LETTER-WRITERS

PAGE 2: BARBARA TO FLORRIE
This is a letter to Florrie Burke, my partner at the time this was written, a woman who matches my energy in work and play. In 1992–93 I took a teaching job in Chicago. Separation inspires me and to keep the connection, I create missives of spontaneous love that often have spelling and punctuation mishaps but are filled with energy like a romantic lover who overlooks defects in her object of desire but lusts after her all the same.

PAGE 34: ELIZABETH TO SANDY
L. and L. have many names. As I write this, they are me and Sandy, the woman I love and who makes me want to write love letters and to dream (sem)erotics. We met in Tuscaloosa, Alabama, in 1988, and have lived here together since 1989. In 1993, we celebrated our 90th birthday (my 50th and her 40th). Both of us teach at the University of Alabama.

This letter is reprinted courtesy of New York University Press from Elizabeth Meese, Sem(erotics): Theorizing Lesbian Writing (New York: NYU Press, 1992).

PAGES 36–37: EMILY TO SUSAN
The American poet, Emily Dickinson, wrote many passionate letters to Susan Gilbert in the mid-19th century. Gilbert eventually married Dickinson's brother. That event seems to have cooled Susan's ardor, but Emily remained devoted for decades. This excerpt is reprinted by permission of the publishers from The Letters of Emily Dickinson, edited by Thomas H. Johnson, Cambridge, MA: The Belknap Press of Harvard University Press, Copyright 1958, 1986 by the President and Fellows of Harvard College.

PAGES 39–40: ISABEL TO ELSA
The long and varied lesbian life of the American poet and writer Elsa Gidlow is recorded in her autobiography I Come With My Songs (Booklegger Publishing, 1986). Three letters written to Elsa by different lovers are published here. This one is from Isabel Quallo. Quallo and Gidlow met and fell in love through correspondence in the late 1940s and eventually lived together in San Francisco in the 1950s.

Used by permission of Booklegger Publishing (Box 460654, San Francisco, CA 94146) and by courtesy of The Gay and Lesbian Historical Society of Northern California.

PAGE 41: HAWLEY TO MERIDITH
In 1993 Hawley Hussey came from San Francisco to spend a month in the Brooklyn heat with Meridith McNeal. Fueled by fifteen years of friendship, we began developing the "Dear Love" project. By now, hundreds of people around the world have become involved in this medium for expressing the joys, and desires, the sorrows and perils to be found on this journey.

PAGES 42–44: JANE TO FLORENCE
Jane Heap, born in Kansas, is best known for her relationship with Margaret Anderson, the founder of the Little Review (1914–29), which published early works by H.D., Eliot, and Joyce. This letter, however, was written to an early lover of Heap's—Florence Reynolds of Chicago, who, until her death in 1949, remained a great and supportive friend to Heap. Permission to reprint courtesy of Karen L. Clark (for Jane Heap's family) and the University of Delaware Library, Florence Reynolds Collection, Newark, Delaware. Special thanks to Dr. Holly Baggett of the University of Utah who is preparing an edition of the Heap–Reynolds correspondence for New York University Press.

PAGES 45–47: LEE TO JOAN
This is one of a series of letters which documents a relationship built on difference. We used the metaphors of geography and climate to speak of our passion and fear of drifting apart. Lee wrote from the "Arctic" and Joan from the "Amazon" even though both of us were actually in New York. Lee Hudson is a jock butch academic government-activist who established the first office for the lesbian and gay community in the Mayor's Office of New York City. Joan Nestle, author/editor of six books including A Restricted Country, is a fifty-six year-old femme New Yorker who co-founded the Lesbian Herstory Archives.

PAGES 48–50: ROSIE TO ANNA
We met first in 1977 at university in England, when Anna was 19, and I was 21. We became involved 4 years later, at the

tail end of 1981, but she broke up with me the following summer. I tried for many years to win her back. Finally I gave up. Then, to my utter astonishment, on 1st January 1993, she declared herself to me again—after ten years!

PAGE 51: MARTHA TO JOAN At the time these letters were written, my lover and I were both forty-eight years old. She had been sexual with women for almost three decades; it was my first time out. Aware of a profound attraction, I approached her (in writing, at first). This note was written when we had been lovers for about two weeks.

PAGES 52—53: RITA TO MARLA During that relationship's instantaneous onset, sizzling duration, and long aftermath, I could have told you every single detail: the number of the Haight Street bus I first spotted Marla standing on, the title of the book inside the plastic bag she toted, the number of keys hanging from her waist, and on and on—our first kiss, our sudden divorce. When she left me, for years I prayed for her return at the magic spot on the sidewalk where we'd exchanged our first breathless words. The gifts of her leaving: I got myself in all my dimensions, and one small hole in my heart my beloved bunny Jane could burrow into, to stay.

PAGES 55—56: BETHROOT TO THYME We were inventing a new world, as part of the emerging lesbian land movement in the 1970s. This letter reminds me of the bold, earnest spirit of those undertakings. This flirtation was a path not taken, but I'm proud of myself for the reaching.

PAGE 58—59: GRETCHEN TO ANN Gretchen Phillips has wanted a tall, sexy, go-go dancing English teacher since she was a kid. Her dream came true when she and Dr. Ann Cvetkovich finally got physical (rather than mental) on September 8, 1991. Since then things have continued to be beautiful and provocative and Gretchen now firmly believes in fate.

PAGES 60—61: THELMA (SIMON) TO DJUNA The American author Djuna Barnes, who wrote the deliciously deviant and legendary *Nightwood*, among other books, lived on the Left Bank in Paris during the 1920s and '30s, then spent the rest of her life in New York. In 1921 she met Thelma Wood, a

striking, booted, six-foot-tall American who became, according to Barnes, "my great love."

This letter is published with permission from the Papers of Djuna Barnes, Special Collections, University of Maryland at College Park Libraries.

PAGES 62—63: LISSA TO MINDIE In 1994 Lissa and Mindie met one afternoon in the Kansas wind and were, from that day forward, born on each other's wings. No matter when you read this, they will be together empowering each other on a gorgeously orchestrated collision course with their own destiny.

PAGES 64—65: LUCINDA TO POLLY Polly and Lucinda met at a Librarian's convention in Washington, D.C. on January 9, 1989. Fortunate to have early and easy access to the internet at their otherwise dull university jobs, they corresponded via e-mail for 8 months until Lucinda moved from Kentucky to join Polly in NYC. They were joint caretakers of the Lesbian Herstory Archives from the time it moved to Brooklyn in June 1992 until their break-up in January 1994. Their e-mail correspondence continues, though it looks quite different today.

PAGES 66—67: LAURA TO MADISON We've been together two years now. We are nurses at Texas Children's Hospital. Madison is very androgynous and I am very femme. I did leave Terry (my partner of 10 years) about two weeks after this letter was written.

PAGES 68—70: M.T. TO K.C. I met K.C. at the Southern Women's Music Festival in 1988 and got a giant festival crush on her. She kissed me once but she had a girlfriend back home. I was tormented, actually went to New York to visit her and her girlfriend only to be tormented some more. But luckily by the next year's festival she was single. Our relationship evolved then it dissolved. She still says I was the nicest girlfriend to ever break up with her.

PAGE 70: ALMEDA TO EMMA Although the exact nature of the relationship between the feminist and union organizer Almeda Sperry and the famous anarchist, writer, and social leader Emma Goldman is unknown, Sperry wrote explicit, eloquent love letters to Goldman in the early part of the 20th century.

Permission to publish is granted courtesy of Boston

University, The Mugar Memorial Library, the Emma Goldman Collection. Other Sperry letters are published by Jonathan Katz in his *Gay American History* (New York: T.Y. Crowell, 1976).

PAGES 72–73: JOAN TO BEBETI An affair between two writers (I am a playwright, she a novelist) from different countries (U.S. and Brazil), complicated by the fact that I had just separated from a lover and she was still living with one. Faute de mieux, the affair was mostly literary (communication by letter) and electronic (communication by fax).

PAGE 74: LOURDES TO ANNETTE Lourdes Perez and Annette D'Armata (the Fifis) met in Houston in 1991. They had a rough time getting to the first date, but once they did, they dated for one week and then moved in together. They have not spent one night apart since. Lourdes is a 34-year-old Puerto Rican recording artist. Annette is a 28-year old Lebanese-Irish/Italian music producer and graphic designer.

PAGES 76–77: TIFFANY TO AUDREY The poem referred to in the letter is "Diving Into the Wreck" by Adrienne Rich. Audrey and Tiffany met in November of 1994 and attempted for almost a year to overcome the communication barrier that stands between all people, hearing people included.

PAGE 78: PAULA TO KATHLEEN

Paula (age 53) and Kathleen (age 52) became lovers at the end of August, 1994, two months after Paula, a sculptor/visual artist, declared in a note to her friend of three years, Kathleen——a poet/short story writer who had been married for thirty-one years——that she was in love with her.

PAGE 79: MARY MARGARET TO JOANNA Jersey Girl meets Texas Swirl. Late into the night they danced. Fifteen years later still bumpin' along. To their sweet Virgin, they give thanks.

PAGE 80: LILLIAN TO MABEL Lillian Foster (1900–78) met Mabel Hampton (1902–89) on a streetcar in New York in 1937. They were together 41 years. Mabel was an active presence in the Lesbian Herstory Arhives.

This letter is courtesy of the Mabel Hampton Collection of the Lesbian Herstory Archives/Lesbian Herstory

Educational Foundation, Inc., New York City.

PAGE 82: ROBIN TO PATRICIA Patricia was 41 and I was 35 when our relationship began in Memphis in April 1993. We met when I answered an ad to house-sit for her. I assume she was satisfied with my work as I never really left after that.

PAGE 83: SUSAN TO REBECCA We were both "fighting crime" in San Francisco in April of 1986. In trying to figure out how to seduce Rebecca, I was advised to take her to the movie "Desert Hearts." Sure enough, the night we saw the movie proved to be our "first time." I was her first woman lover, and I wrote this note to her on the first anniversary of our first night we shared as lovers in April of 1987.

PAGES 84–85: PANTHER (TOMMY) TO ELSA This letter to Elsa Gidlow is from Violet Winifred Leslie Henry-Anderson, known as "Tommy," with whom Elsa became lovers in 1924. The two kept family with several beloved cats and Tommy takes on a cat's identity in many of her letters, signing off as "Panther." She often addressed and characterized Gidlow as the "Dryad" (a nymph who inhabits trees).

Used by permission of Booklegger Publishing (Box 460654, San Francisco, CA 94146) and by courtesy of The Gay and Lesbian Historical Society of Northern Carolina.

PAGES 86–87: CATHERINE TO CRISTINA At the time this letter was written, in 1985, Catherine and Cristina had just separated because Cristina was with someone else. After a long period of readjustment C. and C. have resumed their very close friendship. In fact they roomed together at the Women's Conference in Beijing in September 1995.

PAGES 88–89: TATIANA TO GLORIA Colombian native of the universe living on the edge, tatiana de la tierra is a writer and editor/founder of *conmoción* who currently lives in Miami. She's learned not to drag relationships across continents——something gets lost along the way.

PAGE 90: SUE TO SUSAN "Sue" (known for many years as "Acorn," and then as "Flame") and Susan (now called Shoshana) met in rural southern Oregon on Thanksgiving weekend, 1974. Their relationship flourished during the next year and a half and included two honeymoons and several cross-country trips in Susan's 1972 Valiant (still running!). They were friends until Flame died of cancer in 1994.

PAGES 92–93: CATHY TO MICHELLE Letters are thinking outloud, feeling outloud; the most self-revealing activity I do, the best gift I give myself. And at 46, changes as huge as proclaiming love for my best friend and giving self gifts, need to be outloud.

PAGES 94–96: REBECCA TO CHERESE Cherese Campo and Rebecca Evans met and fell truly, madly, deeply in love in Seattle in 1991. They are now living happily ever after.

PAGE 97: DAILE TO DONNA Donna Henes and Daile Kaplan met in 1978 when Donna replaced Daile as drummer in the women's performance group, *Disband*. Pals for several years until, on the summer solstice, 1981, they were overcome with the desire to *trance*form the nature of their relationship. Central to their idea of romance is the 14-year-long voluminous correspondence which they have maintained——whether across continents or a crowded room.

PAGES 98–99: GIGI TO CAYENNE Cayenne (40 years old) & Gigi (33 years old) fell in love "on-line" before they actually met in September, 1994. Gigi moved from Austin to San Francisco in July 1995 to be with Cayenne. They are deliriously happy in butch/femme heaven.

PAGES 100–01: DEBBIE TO BETH Beth and I met in college in the classic city, Athens, Georgia. This was my coming out, that is first lesbian relationship, though Beth was a seasoned veteran. She was 20; I was 21. We're great friends to this day.

This letter is courtesy of the Lesbian Herstory Archives/ Lesbian Herstory Educational Foundation, Inc., New York City.

PAGES 102–03: RADCLYFFE (JOHN) TO SOULINE Radclyffe Hall (1880–1943), author of *The Well of Loneliness*, was partnered for most of her life with Una Troubridge. But late in life Hall fell in love with a younger woman, Evgenia Souline, a Russian-born nurse who had been hired to care for Lady Una during an illness.

This letter to Souline is published with the permission of both the Harry Ransom Humanities Research Center, The University of Texas at Austin, and the Estate of Radclyffe Hall. Copyright the Estate of Radclyffe Hall.

PAGE 104: ZOFIA TO ANN Ann and Zofia met in the locker room at the women's gym at Cornell University in the fall of 1984. They became lovers in the spring of 1985. Since then their relationship has changed, and the physical distance between them enlarged, but letter-writing still serves as a vehicle for bridging distances.

PAGES 105–06: CHAROULA TO JUDY Charoula fell in love with Judy at Vassar College in the early 1960s. But Judy was a bit of a butterfly, unable to commit. She had a brief affair with Gail and at the same time introduced Charoula to her. Then Gail and Charoula became lovers and they have been together ever since, thirty-three years and counting. In 1968, upon hearing the Beatles' song about aging, Gail wrote to Charoula, "If I love you so much when I'm 31, it is impossible to think of the amount and strength when I'm 64 ..."

PAGE 107: R. TO D. When I wrote this letter, I had a dying marriage, a dying but alive and very loving son, and a beautiful compassionate daughter. I was and am alive with the truth of love and death, and love of life.

PAGES 108–09: JOANNE TO KAY Joanne DeMark, an eternally proud and political lesbian-feminist, wrote love and lust to author Kay Leigh Hagan in 1986, early in their two-year long Atlanta relationship. In the moons since, they have been committed "heart sisters," a practice of lesbian love Kay discusses in her book, *Fugitive Information: Essays from a Feminist Hothead* (Harper San Francisco, 1994).

PAGES 110–11: CELESTE TO ELSA A letter from Celeste West, who in 1985 answered Elsa Gidlow's written request to "Come join me tonight in the Springtime of my death." West is a pansexual, devoted hortiphile and lover of scholarly women, who began writing advice for the love worn in *Lesbian Love Advisor* (Cleis, 1989). West left the garden path for wildflower slopes in *Lesbian Polyfidelity* (Booklegger Publishing, 1996) and is now cloud-hidden, whereabouts unknown.

Used by permission of Booklegger Publishing (Box 460654, San Francisco, CA 94146).

PAGES 112—14: ALLISON TO SHERI This letter from "The Land" is an excerpt from a 20-page testimony of longing obsessively scrawled from the Michigan Womyn's Music Festival during one of the first months of our relationship. We are still together and I am still obsessively scrawling.

PAGES 115—16: MARY TO JEANNETTE Mary Woolley was a professor of Biblical history at Wellesley College when she met a student, Jeannette Marks, in 1895. They courted for five years. At the turn of the century, Woolley became the President of Mt. Holyoke College. This letter was written before Marks was appointed to the college faculty and came to live permanently with Woolley at Holyoke.

Permission to publish from the Papers of Mary Woolley is granted by the Mt. Holyoke College Archives and Special Collections, South Hadley, MA.

PAGES 118—19: STEFANIE TO JUDY I found the womon of my dreams in high school. We thought we were straight. We've loved each other through harassment, illness, poverty, and self-doubt. In May 1995, we celebrated our 10th year together.

PAGES 120—21: MERRY TO RUE ... and with that I rolled ... straight into the lap of this adorable tousle-haired woman. "So," I said looking up at her, "will you have dinner with me?" And she cocked her head to one side, laughed, and ran her fingers through my hair. "Well, all right, but what's your name?"

This is how Rue and Merry met in January of 1990. In November 1995, a marvelous magical ceremony affirming their love preceded the best party they ever had the pleasure to throw.

PAGE 122: WESSELY TO GENA In her worldwide search for a partner who can come in less than an hour, Wessely has lived in too many places. She currently awaits her "bride to be" in Los Angeles. OY. Gena pursued me after catching my cabaret act ...(Never date a fan ...) We moved to New York together shortly before I was admitted to the Betty Ford Center. Once she realized I was unfortunately human

offstage (and addicted to Valium), she lost interest.

PAGES 124: GERTRUDE TO ALICE The writer Gertrude Stein and her lover Alice B. Toklas are certainly preeminent in their status as *the* lesbian couple of the 20th century.

Permission to publish this love note is granted by The Yale Collection of American Literature, The Beinecke Rare Book and Manuscript Library, Yale University and the Estate of Gertrude Stein. Copyright the Estate of Gertrude Stein.

PAGE 125: GAIL TO ROULIE (CHAROULA) See p. 156, Charoula to Judy.

PAGES 126—27: OCEAN TO GLORIA This note is quoted in *Homosexual Practices of Institutionalized Females* by Charles A. Ford and published in the *Journal of Abnormal and Social Psychiatry* in 1929. Ford gives a fairly detailed picture of the way lesbian relationships were introduced and maintained through secretive note-passing in the prison group he studied.

PAGES 128—29: MAY TO ZAN The poet May Swenson and Zan Knudson met while teaching at Purdue University in 1966. In 1967 they bought a house in Sea Cliff, New York, where they lived until May's death on December 4, 1989. May sometimes sent letter/poems to Zan. This example published courtesy of The Literary Estate of May Swenson.

PAGE 130: SARAH TO ANNIE The 19th-century American writer Sarah Orne Jewett lived and loved in a respectable "Boston marriage" with Annie Fields for over thirty years. After Jewett's death in 1909, Fields published a volume of correspondence, *Letters of Sarah Orne Jewett* (Boston: Houghton Mifflin, 1911), from which this excerpt is taken. According to historian Lillian Faderman, Fields was counselled by her advisor, the *Atlantic Monthly* editor Mark DeWolfe Howe, to delete most of the references to affection between the two women. The unexpurgated letters remain unpublished.

PAGES 132—33: CAROLE TO HELEN Carole and Helen met in college and are still together 20 years later. "Their" song is "You're My Thrill" sung by Billie Holiday.

PAGE 134: CHRISTINA TO WENDY Christina Minna spends most of her life touring with the band *Fem 2 Fem.* She met Wendy Jill York, the photographer and current editor of the magazine *50/50,* during an interview. Much of their relationship was conducted via letters and faxes—the example published here is a fax—sent back and forth while Christina was on the road.

PAGES 136–37: DEZ TO TRUDY Dez lives for lesbian love, a hit of pot, and a good crap shoot.

PAGES 138–39: MARGARET TO LOUISE In the early 1960s, two antique hunters—a mother and daughter team—purchased an old picture frame that was bulging in the back with what they hoped might be hidden and forgotten money. In fact the frame was filled with love letters written by Margaret to Louise when the two were separated for a period in 1913. The mother was shocked and told her daughter to destroy the letters. But for some reason the daughter disobeyed. When her stepdaughter, Nancy Morgan, came out as a lesbian twenty years later, the letters were transferred to her. Morgan traced the story of the letter-writers in her Senior Thesis (University of Santa Cruz, 1984).

PAGES 140, 142: BARBARA TO JAN Barbara Lee, R.N., left her cushy publishing career of twenty years to become a critical care nurse in 1995. Her current love letters are written to Florence, *la donna stupenda.* Twenty years after writing the letter published here she remains friends with its recipient, Jan, the woman who almost ...

PAGE 143: JANICE TO CONI Janice 36, Coni 38. Monogamous long-distance relationship, seeded in June '94, bloomed Aug. '94 at the Michigan Womyn's Music Festival. It's all that, and a bag of chips!

PAGES 144–45: Y. TO D. The writer requires anonymity.

PAGE 146: DANA TO CELESTE Celeste was 35 and I was 32. We both lived in San Francisco at the time this letter was written. Both of us had attended Catholic school as children and Celeste still enjoyed wearing those pleated black skirts, but a tad shorter than she or I were allowed back in the golden rule days. I was kneeling on the floor and Celeste was sitting on the bed wearing this mini skirt when our first kiss miraculously occurred. I later realized this day was Ash Wednesday and the letter along with our relationship is now history.

PAGES 148–49: JAN TO BJ Poised on transition points of age (I was 39, she was 29), our relationship really began at a 1982 Winter Solstice gathering in New Brunswick NJ when BJ surprised me with a warm goodbye kiss. Thirteen years later we continue. Recently, on the dunes of North Truro, we exchanged rings as a token of our commitment pledging, "I will love you forever even if I tell people I don't."

PAGE 150: L. TO LEILA The writer requires anonymity.

This letter is courtesy of the Lesbian Herstory Archives/Lesbian Herstory Educational Foundation, Inc., New York City.

PAGE 152: VIRGINIA TO VITA The British writer Virginia Woolf met another British writer Vita Sackville-West on December 14, 1922. In her journal Woolf described Vita as a "grenadier; hard; handsome; manly ..." who made her feel "virgin, shy & schoolgirlish ..." Woolf admitted her infatuation with this "pronounced Sapphist" and remained devoted to Vita for the rest of her life. The letters which document the peak moments of their affair, and from which this letter is taken, are found in *The Letters of Virginia Woolf,* Vol. 3, edited by Nigel Nicholson and Joanna Trautmann.

This letter in its original is archived in the Berg Collection of the New York Public Library, New York City. Permission to reproduce the letter is granted by the Estate of Virginia Woolf, Chatto & Windus, London, and Harcourt Brace & Co. in the U.S.A.

ACKNOWLEDGMENTS

A project of this kind is assembled piece by piece, one letter at a time. It is the kind of project that depends upon the interest and kindness of many, including the friends, colleagues, lovers, and strangers mentioned here. I owe a love letter to: Mary Sanger, Nancy Dean, my personal assistant Lisa Graybill, Karen Dinitz, Judy Adkins, Rita S. Losch, Jane Sneed, Elizabeth Meese, Ann Cvetkovich, the 96th Street Posse (Rikki and Ed), Randy and David, Martha Barnette and Deb Clem, Gerard Koskovich, Jonathan Katz, Susan Kay Gilbert, Janice Babula, Cherese Campo, Rebecca Evans, Margot and Maria, Christine Reed, Allison "Tex" Clark, Susan Sweet-Scott, Jimmy and Barbara Turner, The Lesbian Herstory Archives (PO Box 1258, New York, NY 10116), and especially Polly Thistlethwaithe, Dez, and Joan Nestle, The Gay and Lesbian Historical Society of Northern California (PO BOX 424280, San Francisco, CA 94142), Degania Golove and the June Mazer Lesbian Collection (626 N. Robertson, West Hollywood, CA 90069), Janice Uhlman and The Ohio Lesbian Archive (4039 Hamilton Ave., Cincinnati, OH 45223), Gerber/Hart Gay and Lesbian Archives (3352 N. Paulina St., Chicago, IL 60657), Feminist Bookstore Newsletter, Celeste West and Booklegger Publishing (PO Box 460654, San Francisco, CA 94146), Katherine Sadler of Widdershins Books, Susan Post of Bookwoman, Audrey May of Meristem Books, Sisterhood Bookstore, Old Wives' Tales, In Other Words Bookstore, Lynn Frost of The Women's Project in Little Rock, AR, Amy Edgington, Kathie Bergquist, Cynthia White, Garbo at Fan the Flames, Colleen at Crazy Ladies, Kelley at Common Language Books, River at Pandora Books, Women and Children First, Gabrielle Winkler, Jan Solari, Holly Baggett, Karla Jay, and the staff of Thames and Hudson. Most of all, thanks to all the women everywhere who sent me letters and shared with me their herstory of lesbian love.

COLLAGE CREDITS

Unless otherwise stated, all collages are by Sheri Tornatore and Kay Turner. Page numbers are in bold.

1 Love plastic frame/Forever tattoo/Self-portrait of Lez Nez (Kathy and Allison), 1995. **2** Original letter in the form of a photo-collage by Barbara Hammer. **5–7** Ad image, c. 1960/Postcard, Country Lasses, c. 1915/Photo of Alix and Retts, 1994. **8** Top: Lithograph after Venus Verticordia, painting by Dante Gabriel Rossetti, 1864–68/Photo: Carol's Garden of Love, by Kathy Waldron, 1991/Color-copied Valentine message candies. **33** Liquor advertisement, c. 1975/Photo: Lynn and Gigi's Cafe Life, by Carlos Ramirez, 1995. **35** Collage by Rita S. Losch,

1992—samples from a plumber's supply catalog/Smiley face/ Woman's profile/Venus-goddess figure. **36–37** Answers/ Questions painting by Linda Stanton, 1986/Photo of Susan Gilbert Dickinson, c. 1851, The Houghton Library of the Harvard College Library/Catalog image. **38** The Lyric Movie Theater, New York City, photo: David Kolwyck, 1994/Photos of Elsa Gidlow: 1924 (left) and 1965 (right) courtesy of Booklegger Publishing, 1983 (center) by Marcelina Martin. **41** Collage by Meridith McNeal, 1995—incense package, 1995/Photos of Meridith and Allison/Pen and ink, watercolor embellishments. **43** Stamps/Japanese paper/Sun & Girls, engraving, 19th. c./Wrapping paper/Crown from children's encyclopedia, c. 1960/Attached aluminum foil ditties. **47** Top photo: Ruth and Susan by Jill Guttman, 1991/Center: Liz and Sandy, photobooth pic., 1990s/Bottom: snapshot of Carol and Joan, early 1960s. **49** World stamps/Photo: the Rose family of Arizona, 1995. **51** Collage by Gail Wallat—engraving from a horticulture book, 19th c./Gouache painting of traditional Belgian folk puppet figure, Nanesse. **53** Roman copy of a Greek Venus/Postcard Las Vegas, c. 1970/Rendering of a brownstone window. **57** Photo, Arizona desert, c. 1955/Mixed media postcard and catalog cut-outs/Handwritten messages. **59** Head of Cleopatra/Red Pegasus from a Valentine invitation/Cover (detail) of Cartas Amorosas, a Mexican handbook for writing love letters, c. 1985/Silkscreen fragment, c. 1975. **61** Postcard photo, c. 1910/Monte Carlo casino tableau from Prom Night, Lubbock, TX, 1981, with additional cut-outs. **63** Ad for Madame Dean's corsets, 1885/Photo: Dyke Action Machine! Carrie Moyer and Sue Schaffner, 1993. **65** Photogravure of Portrait of Simonetta Vespucci (Städel Institute, Frankfurt) and Portrait of a Woman (Pitti Palace, Florence), by Sandro Botticelli, 15th c./Rubber stamp. **67** Marbled paper from book cover, 19th c./Smoking girlfriends, Lisa and Andrea, photo by Rod, 1991/Photo portrait, c. 1890. **69** Postcard, Bridgewater Diner, Bridgewater, N.J., late 1970s/Photo: by Bud of Lez Nez, 1992. **71** Book marbling (enlarged)/Girl combing hair from an educational study sheet, Mexico, D.F., c. 1970/Photo: Carol at women's festival by Allison Faust, 1985. **73** Oranges, photo by Susan Plum, 1992/Peaches from canned peaches label, c. 1930/Peach pit photo by Kathy Smith, 1995. **75** Martian landscape photo from NASA/Grace and Anne, painting by Debra Clem, 1993/La Maja Desnuda by Francisco de Goya, 1797–98, Prado Museum, Madrid. **77** Engraving of trapeze artist, early 20th c./Woman falling, 19th c. erotic photo with added hippie hair. **79** Sacred Heart of Mary, holy card, early 20th c./Original letter from Mary Margaret Návar to Joanna Labow, 1980/Virgin of Guadalupe rubber stamp, 1990s. **81** Letter: Lorraine Foster to Mabel Hampton, c.1946/Photo of Mabel and Lorraine, c. 1970/Hand-decorated envelope, late 1940s. All courtesy of Lesbian Herstory Archives,

New York City. **83** Copy of original letter by Susan Kay to Rebecca, 1987. **85** Holy card for San Ramón (detail)/Venus of Malta, c. 4000 B.C./Head of "Louise" (1977–95), photo by Kay Turner, 1990. **87** Artemis, Roman copy of a Greek statue/Greek ruins in Turkey/Hand-colored pen and ink drawing of *Lulu #3*, the VW van, by Mi Ok Song Bruining, 1994. **89** Mexican postcard, c. 1970/Detail from *The Birth of Venus* by Sandro Botticelli, c. 1482, Uffizi Gallery, Florence. **91** Starch advertisement (manipulated), c. 1940. **93** Wallpaper, late 19th c./Egg detail from *The Garden of Earthly Delights*, Hieronymus Bosch, c. 1510, Prado Museum, Madrid/Photogravure of *Giovanna Degli Albizzi Receives the Gifts of the Four Cardinal Virtues* (detail) by Sandro Botticelli, 15th c., The Louvre, Paris. **95** Color-copied wedding cake figures (manipulated)/Japanese origami paper. **97** Imaginary stamps made from an old dictionary, c. 1920. **99** Photo: Pyramid and Sandy, c. 1989 by Jill Guttman/Detail of advertisement for Madame Dean's corsets, 1885. **101** Gustave Courbet, *Women Asleep*, 1866, Musée du Petit Palais, Paris/Photo: Beth Levine and Debbie Friedman, San Diego, CA, 1976. **103** Engravings of astrological figures, elements and maps, 18th c./Watercolor, ink, and acrylic montage, *The Dance of Butch and Femme*, by Sheri Tornatore, 1987. **104** Letter fragment, Zofia to Ann, 1986/Paisley giftwrap/Sheet music, *Keep It A Secret*/Portrait of a queen/Hands, detail from 19th-c. trade card/Dot Band-Aid/Pink sewing trim. **107** Photo: erotic nude, 19th c./Shells from an identification book, c. 1960. **109** Collage by Rita S. Losch, 1992— advertising images for ladies' hosiery, c. 1940. **111** Edouard Manet, *Olympia*, 1863, Musée d' Orsay, Paris/Titian, *The Venus of Urbino* (detail), 1538, Uffizi Gallery, Florence, Italy. **113** Michigan map/Bird cut-outs from greeting card, c. 1955/Pen and ink drawings of festival dykes by Karen Porter from a series, *Greetings from the Land*, 1990. **116** Photo: Mary Woolley and Jeannette Marks, Courtesy of Mt. Holyoke College Archives and Special Collections. **117** Postcard image, 1910/Fragment of a letter from Mary Woolley to Jeannette Marks, 1900. Courtesy of Mt. Holyoke College Archives and Special Collections. **118** Air

mail envelope, 1956/Fake snow-globe collage with postcard photo insert/Foil ditties/Liquid Paper dots. **121** Envelope interior (enlarged)/Hands from detergent ad, c. 1955/Trade card in the form of a letter, c. 1900. **123** Computer-derived background/Photogravure of *Maria Madalena*, by Carlo Crivelli, 15th c., Rijksmuseum, Amsterdam/Vibrator from *Eve's Garden* catalog, c. 1980. **124** Postcard, *Girl Crossing*, c. 1970, Collection of Don and Newly Preziosi/Postcard, dancing maidens, c. 1910. **127** Photo: *My Favorite Loafers*, Dixie Sheridan/Photo: Gladys Bentley, lesbian musician c. 1930. From the postcard collection of Mimi Yahn. **129** Collage by Rita S. Losch, 1991— various ad images: ice cream, hand, and chess piece. **131** Icon frame/Round frame (detail)/Marble leaves and flowers (architectural detail)/Rose collage/Clock-sundial from an invitation/Color copy of handmade photo-pin purchased at women's festival, 1989. **133** *The Genealogy of Lesbian Heads*, mixed media, photos by permission of living lesbians. **135** Collage by Laura Cobb, 1994—photos/Passport/Stamps/Letter excerpt. **137** Engraving of a vulva from the frontispiece of Félix Nogaret's *L' Arétin Francais*, 1787/Details (manipulated) of a painting attributed to Achille Deveria, mid-19th c. Gichner Foundation for Cultural Studies. **139** Moon from an educational study sheet, Mexico, D.F., c. 1970/Painting, unidentified salon, 19th c. **141** Wallpaper, c. 1940/Seaside vacation postcard (detail), c. 1910/*Hotel Menses* stationery by David Kolwyck, 1987. **143** Photo: *Coni and Janice* by Kay Turner, 1995/Screen print, c. 1970. **145** Celestial backdrop, illustration from stargazer's guide, c. 1960/Photo: Degania Goldman and "Ron," San Francisco, 1947/Ad image Empire Dress Shields, c. 1945. **147** Wallpaper, early 20th c./Mixed image fragments from Hieronymus Bosch, *The Garden of Earthly Delights*, c. 1510, Prado Museum, Madrid. **149** Collage by B. J. Ryan, 1994— lace/Excerpts cut from letter to Jan Cunning/Handmade paper hearts. **151** Collage by Kay Yourist and Susan Minard, 1995—Bullseye/Illustration of a heart/Photo of a riveter, c. 1940. **152** Postcard images, c. 1920/Watercolored tissue paper by Sheri Tornatore.